ENERGY

PHYSICS IN ACTION

Energy

Forces and Motion

The Nature of Matter

Planets, Stars, and Galaxies

Processes That Shape the Earth

PHYSICS in ACTION

ENERGY

Andrew Dean Foland, Ph.D.

Series Editor
David G. Haase

CHELSEA HOUSE
PUBLISHERS
An imprint of Infobase Publishing

Energy
Copyright © 2007 by Infobase Publishing

Chelsea House
An imprint of Infobase Publishing
132 West 31st Street
New York NY 10001

Library of Congress Cataloging-in-Publication Data
Foland, Andrew Dean.
 Energy / Andrew Dean Foland, Ph.D.
     p. cm. — (Physics in action)
 Includes bibliographical references and index.
 ISBN-13: 978-0-7910-8930-9 (hardcover)
 ISBN-10: 0-7910-8930-4 (hardcover)
 1. Force and energy. I. Title. II. Series.
 QC73.F65 2007
 531'.6—dc22   2007009055

Chelsea House books are available at special discounts when purchased in bulk quantities for businesses, associations, institutions, or sales promotions. Please call our Special Sales Department in New York at (212) 967-8800 or (800) 322-8755.

You can find Chelsea House on the World Wide Web at http://www.chelseahouse.com

Text design by James Scotto-Lavino
Cover design by Ben Peterson

Printed in the United States of America

Bang NMSG 10 9 8 7 6 5 4 3 2

This book is printed on acid-free paper.

All links and Web addresses were checked and verified to be correct at the time of publication. Because of the dynamic nature of the Web, some addresses and links may have changed since publication and may no longer be valid.

Contents

1 What Is Energy?. 7

2 Kinetic Energy of a Skater: 5,000 Joules . . . 18

3 Potential Energy of Liberty's Torch:
3.4 Million Joules 35

4 Heat Power of the Sun in 1 m²:
1,500 Watts 52

5 Electrical Energy of an AA Battery:
8 Watt-Hours 65

6 Chemical Energy of 1 Kilogram of Sugar:
17 Million Joules 77

7 Relativistic Energy of 1 Kilogram of
Helium Fusion: 270 Trillion Joules 87

8 Household Energy Use: 43 Kilowatt-Hours . . 98

9 Conclusion 109

Glossary. 111

Bibliography 116

Further Reading 117

Index 120

CHAPTER 1

What Is Energy?

Everyone has heard of energy. We know it is related to the cars we drive, the lights we turn on at night, or the food we cook for dinner. Most of us feel that it is somehow related to power. We also use the word *energy* to describe a person ("very energetic") or vague feelings (for instance, someone might say, "I sense an energy here").

In everyday life, it is perfectly acceptable to use the word *energy* in these various ways. In physics, though, energy is a precisely defined idea. Unfortunately, it is easy to confuse the everyday meanings of energy with its technical definition. It is also unfortunate that many explanations of energy in physics are either confusing or incorrect.

So, it will be helpful, first, to make a list of things that are not energy. Most of these things have something to do with energy, but they are not energy. The distinction will make it much easier to understand what energy is.

- Energy is not electricity.
- Energy is not a force.
- Energy is not sunlight.

- Energy is not oil.
- Energy is not a fluid.
- Energy is not power.
- Energy is not radiation.
- Energy is not infrared light.

In short, energy is not any material object at all. Material objects can have or carry energy but themselves are not energy. In this way, energy is sort of like the idea of color: objects have colors, but color is not an object. If you could imagine a slightly kooky bumper-car amusement park ride where the cars could exchange their colors whenever they collided, you would have a good start toward understanding energy. A car might, for instance, carry "redness" from one place to another, much like light carries energy from one place to another.

Another common definition of energy is "the capacity to do work," where "work" is defined within physics. This definition is largely correct; the student who thinks of energy this way will have a fair grasp of the concept. But in some contexts, especially in biology, it is a little bit incomplete, and we will point this out.

Regardless of what energy is, we will learn in this book how to calculate the amount of energy there is in many situations—and once you have calculated the amount of energy there is in a situation, then the total amount of energy calculated must always stay the same, even if the situation changes. That is, the situation is only allowed to change to another situation with the same amount of calculated energy. This is what we mean when we say, "Energy is always conserved." According to the law of **conservation**, energy cannot be created or destroyed—the calculated amount cannot go up or down.

Energy comes in many forms, and at bottom, all forms of energy share the same principles. Nonetheless, the formula used to calculate the amount of energy differs from one situation to another. In the course of this book, we will see many of these forms: from the fundamental definition of energy to mechanical energy, potential energy, heat energy, electrical energy, chemical energy, and nuclear energy.

Wolfgang Pauli and Conservation of Energy

Physicists believe so strongly in the conservation of energy that one physicist once used it to predict the existence of a brand new particle. In 1930, Wolfgang Pauli was considering the recently discovered radioactive decay of elements that emitted gamma rays. Measurements had revealed that when these elements underwent transformations, the total energy afterwards was less than it had been before the transformation. This was quite puzzling to physicists of the time, as it violated the law of conservation of energy. Professor Pauli wrote the following letter on December 4 of that year:

> Dear Radioactive Ladies and Gentlemen,
>
> As the bearer of these lines, to whom I graciously ask you to listen, will explain to you in more detail, how because of the "wrong" statistics of the N and Li^6 nuclei and the continuous beta spectrum, I have hit upon a desperate remedy to save the "exchange theorem" of statistics and the law of conservation of energy. Namely, the possibility that there could exist in the nuclei electrically neutral particles, that I wish to call neutrinos. . . .
>
> I agree that my remedy could seem incredible because one should have seen these neutrinos much earlier if they really exist. But only the ones who dare can win. . . .

His suggestion of neutrinos meant the particles were invisible and non-interacting—unlike any other particle known before or since. Pauli's "desperate remedy," however, quickly became accepted as the theoretical solution to the problem. In 1956, these particles were directly detected for the first time, confirming the hypothesis.

Let us now come back to the question of "what energy is." It would be fairest to say, "Energy is a useful number that you can calculate in any physics situation, and the total number will never change thereafter." This is a little unsatisfying if you were hoping for a statement like "energy is a fluid" or "energy is the motion of little tiny particles." Unfortunately, energy is an abstract quantity, and a slightly absurd and complicated one at that. As the Swiss theorist Wolfgang Pauli is rumored to have said, "Just shut up and calculate!" It is useful to recall the words of the great Richard Feynman, in his book QED: *The Strange Theory of Light and Matter*:

> It is not a question of whether a theory is philosophically delightful, or easy to understand, or perfectly reasonable from the point of view of common sense. The theory . . . describes Nature as absurd from the point of view of common sense. And it agrees fully with experiment.

All that said, though, if you feel cheated in learning what energy is, you can fall back on our earlier statement, "Energy is the capacity to do work."

You might wonder, then, "Why is it that the number never changes thereafter?" This has a somewhat cleaner answer. The physicist Emmy Noether proved that if the laws of physics are the same today as they were yesterday, then the energy must be conserved. So, the energy number never changes from one situation to another because the laws of physics do not change from day to day. This fact is by no means obvious—figuring it out is why Ms. Noether became famous.

MEASURING ENERGY

You may understand in general that a speeding truck has more energy than a butterfly does, or that a gallon of gasoline can provide more energy to a car than a gallon of water would. But how are these energies measured? We seldom have an "energy meter" that reads out the answer. Usually the energy of an object is calculated from quantities such as the object's speed, mass, or position.

Just as length is measured in feet or meters, and time is measured in seconds, energy must also be measured in some system of

Emmy Noether

For most of the nineteenth century and part of the twentieth century, physicists could not understand why energy was conserved. It was regarded as an important experimental fact without theoretical understanding. The reason for the conservation of energy was discovered in 1918 by Emmy Noether (1882–1935). In fact, she discovered the basis for all known conservation laws (including, for instance, conservation of momentum). Her most famous physics theorem (known as Noether's theorem) is considered one of the most important foundations for advanced physics today. This theorem says that every conservation law is the consequence of symmetry in the laws of physics.

For instance, the laws of physics have time symmetry—they are the same every day. This time symmetry leads to conservation of energy. They also have space symmetry—they are the same here as they are in China or on Mars. This space symmetry leads to conservation of momentum. The laws of physics are also the same whether you stand normally or on your head—they have rotation symmetry. This leads to a conservation law called conservation of angular momentum.

It wasn't easy for Noether to pursue her talents. Despite discovering a physics law of great depth and power (it is less famous than, but similar in importance to, the theory of relativity), women in her time were not allowed to be professors in universities in Germany. Her talents were so great, however, and her supporters (including Albert Einstein) so vocal, that she overcame this prejudice and was eventually allowed both to earn a Ph.D. and to accept a teaching position at the University of Erlangen.

units. There are four common units in use for measuring energy— we will encounter three of them in this book, and the fourth (BTU) is commonly used in everyday life. The official energy unit of the SI system (the International System of Units, now used for most scientific purposes) is the **joule** (abbreviated "J"). One joule is twice as much as the mechanical energy (described in the next chapter) carried by a one-kilogram object moving at one meter per second. One joule is about the amount of energy you exert in lifting a cup of water from the table to your mouth.

Another unit of energy, which we will use very little in the book, is the calorie. The definition of a calorie is the amount of energy that will raise the temperature of one gram of water by one degree Celsius. One calorie is approximately 4.2 joules. A more commonly used term is the **Calorie** (note the capital "C"). One Calorie is 1,000 calories, and thus it is also known as the kilocalorie. A Diet Coke, with only one Calorie, actually carries 4,200 joules of energy (Figure 1.1).

In describing the motion of atoms and molecules, we use a very small unit of energy—the **electron volt** (eV). Although electricity is itself not energy, we will see that electrical fields can increase or decrease the energy of charged particles such as **electrons**. Batteries are rated in volts—for instance, a 9-volt battery—that tell how much work the battery will do on an electron. If one electron travels from the negative terminal to the positive terminal of a 9-volt battery, it ends up carrying off 9 electron volts of energy from the battery. If two electrons travel, their total energy is 18 electron volts. Of course, one electron is very small, so one electron volt is very little energy: 1.6×10^{-19} J.

Finally, the English system of units uses the **BTU** (British thermal unit). We will have little use for this unit in the book, but it is common enough in daily life that it deserves some explanation. One BTU is equal to 1,055 joules. So, a 5,000-BTU/hour air conditioner removes 5,275,000 joules of energy from a room in one hour. Such an air conditioner is generally sufficient for a small room, while a 500,000-BTU/hour A/C unit might cool an entire building. (Note that everyone says "BTU" for measuring air conditioner output, but BTU per hour is the correct unit.)

When should you use each of these units? Of course, in principle, it doesn't matter. The length of the movie *The Fellowship of the Ring* is the same whether you call it 3 hours, 180 minutes,

Figure 1.1 *Measured energy in everyday products. The latest weapon in the battle against weight gain is a 100-Calorie-sized serving of popular drinks, such as this can of Coca-Cola. In food labeling, the term "calorie" usually refers to the kilocalorie.*

or 10,800 seconds. We know, however, that sometimes one set of units are more convenient than another. A set of blueprints would tell you the distance across a living room in feet, but a map would tell you the distance from Los Angeles to New York in miles.

In the same way, joules, Calories, or electron volts could all be used to express the energy carried by something. We'll see, however, that when discussing mechanical energies of "people-sized" things, it is most convenient to use joules. When discussing chemical substances or heat, Calories are common. And when discussing the energy of just a few atoms or electrons, we will use electron volts.

Units and Conversions

You are probably familiar with the SI system of units. In this system, lengths are measured in meters, masses in kilograms, and time in seconds. Together with scientific notation, this set of units allows scientists to communicate unambiguously to one another about the sizes of things. Of course, you know it does not matter whether you measure something in feet or meters—it's the same length. That is always true with units.

If you always carefully write out the units when you are doing a calculation, then it will be much easier to do it correctly. It will take a little more time to do it this way, but it will save you a lot of trouble (and more time) down the road.

There are also "compound" units, such as the joule or watt. However, these can be written as follows:

$$1 \text{ J} = 1 \text{ kg m}^2/\text{s}^2$$
$$1 \text{ W} = 1 \text{ J/s} = 1 \text{ kg m}^2/\text{s}^3$$

When doing a problem, remember that you can always "multiply by one." So, to convert centimeters into meters:

$$200 \text{cm} = 200 \,\cancel{\text{cm}} \times \frac{1\text{m}}{100 \,\cancel{\text{cm}}} = \frac{200}{100}\text{m} = 2\text{m}$$

This method will keep you from having to remember whether to divide by 100 or to multiply when converting numbers.

You will find it best if, when you receive a problem, you first convert it into the SI system. Then you can go ahead and use the various formulas as they were meant to be used. Otherwise, you might forget to convert one of them later.

MEASURING POWER

Power and energy are related, but how? **Power** is defined as the amount of energy absorbed, transformed, or transmitted per second. The air conditioning BTU/hour is a unit of power. The basic SI unit for power is joules per second; this is also known as the **watt** (abbreviated W). The amount of energy used by a light bulb, for instance, is measured in watts, because it is always using energy, a certain amount every second. A 60-watt light bulb transforms 60 joules of energy every second from being carried by electric fields (in the electrical wires of your house) to being carried by light (which you see) and **heat**. (The watt does not measure the amount of light the light bulb puts out. In general, the more power the bulb uses, the more light it emits, but it is possible for two light bulbs with the same power consumption to be of different brightness, or two light bulbs of the same brightness to have different power consumption.)

In addition to the watt, a common unit of power consumption is horsepower: 1 HP is 746 J/s, or 746 W. The horsepower unit was invented so that early steam engine builders could compare their engines to the horse-drawn competition.

A couple of useful points to remember about power. First, if the energy is not changing form (or at least moving from one object to another), then the power is zero. For instance, if an object has 70 J of energy when it travels for 10 seconds, the power during the flight is not 70 J ÷ 10 sec = 7 W. There may be a burst of power (to project the object) at the beginning, or at the end (when the energy comes to a stop and transforms into something else, such as heat), but in between there is no power because no energy is being transformed or transferred.

Second, very powerful processes may involve very little energy, or very energetic processes may involve very little power. It depends on the amount of time the process takes. For instance, every so often a rock falls into the Grand Canyon; as we will see later, this transforms energy from potential to kinetic to heat. It happens rarely enough that the power—energy ÷ time—is very low. But over geologic time (millions of years), the amount of total energy transformed in this way is very large. Similarly, some very powerful lasers can temporarily achieve gigantic power—even up to one billion watts! But they are active only for a trillionth of a second. So, the total energy is only a few thousandths of a joule— roughly the amount of energy it takes you to lift your finger one centimeter off the table.

HOW A PHYSICIST THINKS ABOUT ENERGY

One of the central facts about the world is that it is not possible to create or destroy energy at will. This underlies many of the great debates of our day. It makes the nation that possesses oil reserves both rich and influential. It makes the creator of waste heat potentially dangerous. It makes the nuclear-armed nation vastly more powerful than those who rely on more conventional forms of energy.

At the same time, energy underlies many of the great advances of our day. The storage of energy in batteries makes possible a lifestyle at once mobile and electronic. The simple expedient of finding a high-energy liquid (gasoline) lets us move from place to place quickly, efficiently and in comfort. This book was written on a laptop computer dependent on the energy stored in light, efficient batteries.

It is amusing to consider for a moment how the world might be if this were not the case. How would the world change if energy could be created or destroyed at will? The world would be a much more fantastical place, but it would also be much more unpredictable and chaotic. In short, it might become incomprehensible.

As we will see in this book, energy is a great organizing concept for understanding how the world works. We will see what energy is, the forms it takes, and how to recognize and measure it. We will see that it is simultaneously abstract and concrete. And by the time we are done, we should have a good understanding of just how much of it there is.

Each chapter of this book is organized by a single quantity that will help the reader understand the scale of energy in some common, everyday situations. After having read the book, readers hopefully will be able to use these quantities consistently. It is also hoped that the reader, having completed the book, will understand the words of Thomas Huxley that "Science is simply common sense at its best; that is, rigidly accurate in observation, and merciless to fallacy in logic." Perhaps you'll see science as something you can use as a tool every day, as an extension of common sense. Science is not a mystical, separate kind of knowledge attained by scientists, but simply knowledge.

CHAPTER 2

Kinetic Energy of a Skater: 5,000 Joules

LET'S BEGIN BY TACKLING THE EASIEST SITUATION IN WHICH to calculate the quantity of energy present. This kind of energy is called **kinetic energy**. An object that is in motion is carrying energy simply due to its motion. This means that a moving object can be brought to rest, and this energy of motion could be converted to another form of energy. As we will see in later chapters, it often is converted into forms such as potential energy, heat, or electrical energy.

Most things in motion in everyday life, as you know, tend to slow down. This is due to friction (or one of its forms, such as air resistance). As an object slows down, its kinetic energy must decrease. This energy must go somewhere—and as we will see, it is transformed into heat.

This indicates that we should start off by considering a friction-free environment in order to understand the energy of motion by itself. For instance, on a newly Zamboni-ed surface of ice in a rink, the friction on a skater is very low. In this case, the rule of conservation of energy implies that the kinetic energy of the skater will not really change from one moment to the next.

What do we think might possibly relate to the energy of a skater's motion? Let us just try to think about some possible answers first, before getting to the right answers. You would probably guess that the color of the skater's outfit doesn't change the energy, but the speed of the skater probably does. From your own experience, you know that your muscles work harder to throw a baseball than a ping-pong ball, so you might expect that size or mass of the moving object are related to its energy. You might think the shape of the skater's skates mattered, or the shape of their hat, or whether the skater is skating sideways or forwards. Or you might think that if the skater wears very heavy skates or very light ones, it changes the energy.

But it turns out that to calculate the energy carried by a moving object, we need to know only two things: the total mass of the object and the **speed** of the object. This probably makes sense to you—the bigger and faster the object, the more energy of motion it has.

Suppose the mass of the object is m and the speed of the object is v (for **velocity**); then the kinetic energy (KE) is:

$$KE = \frac{1}{2}mv^2$$

For the moment, you can think of this as simply a fact about our universe, although in the next chapter we will see a way to figure this out for yourself.

A very fast bike rider, such as Lance Armstrong in the Tour de France, might reach speeds of 15 m/s (about 35 miles per hour). If his mass is 45 kg, we can calculate the energy of motion as the biker is riding:

$$KE = \frac{1}{2}mv^2 = \frac{1}{2} \times 45kg \times \left(15\frac{m}{s}\right)^2 = 5,062kg\frac{m^2}{s^2}$$

So, let us examine the units of kinetic energy. Velocity is measured in meters per second, and mass is measured in kilograms. The units of kinetic energy, then, are kilograms × meters²/seconds². In fact, this is the unit of any kind of energy. Because this unit comes up so often, it has its own name, the joule. Joules are the same thing as kg m²/s². A joule is an example of a compound unit, because it is derived from a combination of other units.

Compound units are not found in the simplest things we measure, such as time (measured just in seconds), length (meters), or mass (kilograms). You may already know another compound unit, used in **force**, which is called the **newton**. Force is the mass multiplied by acceleration ($F = ma$). The newton is kg m/s². Velocity is also a compound unit, since it involves both meters and seconds.

In calculating physical properties it is often best to convert compound units to their simplest versions. For example, if you want to use the joule in a problem, be sure to convert all the units to kilograms, meters, and seconds. One kilogram centimeter²/hour² is not a joule.

It is worth noticing that a one kilogram mass moving at one meter per one second does not have the energy of one joule. It has units of joules, but to calculate the energy, we must multiply

$$KE = \frac{1}{2}mv^2$$

If you multiply this out, with one kilogram and one meter per second, you find

$$KE = \frac{1}{2}mv^2 = \frac{1}{2} \times 1kg \times \left(1\frac{m}{s}\right)^2 = \frac{1}{2}kg\frac{m^2}{s^2} = \frac{1}{2}J$$

The somewhat startling thing about kinetic energy is that it depends on the square of the velocity. So, your car, when it travels at 60 miles per hour (27 m/s) has four times as much kinetic energy as when it travels at 30 miles per hour (14 m/s). The skater has four times as much energy of motion when traveling at top speed (15 m/s) as when skating at half-speed (7.5 m/s).

Finally, you've probably heard a great deal about vectors. That is, forces, accelerations, and velocities have not only a size (magnitude) but also a direction. Energy of any sort, including

Signifying Changes with Delta

It is a very common occurrence in physics problems that we have a quantity x, and we would like to examine changes in the quantity x. We need a consistent way to indicate that we are examining the change in a quantity.

The change in the quantity is the difference in the quantity; unless noted otherwise, it is the final value minus the initial quantity. For instance, the change in x is $x_{final} - x_{initial}$. In order to consistently signify this meaning, we use the Greek letter for "d" ("difference"). This is the letter Δ (**delta**). Whenever you see the letter Δ in front of a variable, you know it means the final minus initial values:

$$\Delta x = x_{final} - x_{initial}$$
$$\Delta E = E_{final} - E_{initial}$$
$$\Delta t = t_{final} - t_{initial}$$

kinetic energy, does not have a direction. It is just a single number (magnitude) that you calculate. In physics, such quantities are sometimes called scalars. For instance, temperature is just temperature, just a number. You might calculate the number as Fahrenheit or Celsius, but when you're done, it's a number, saying only how warm or cold it is. On the other hand, a force not only has a magnitude (saying how strong it is) but also a direction. For instance, the gravitational force at the surface of the Earth always points downward.

WORK

Energy also measures **work**. Although you probably think of work as anything you have to do that you don't like, in physics there is a precise definition of work. Work is about exerting a force that makes an object move a distance. The work you do is the force

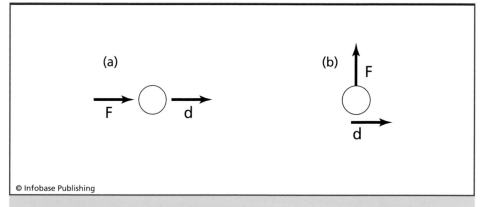

Figure 2.1 *(a) Force is in the same direction as displacement, the most common situation. The force vector and displacement vector have an angle of zero degrees. (b) Force is perpendicular to the motion. This is the case for twirling a weight on a rope. The angle between the force and the displacement is zero.*

times the distance (also known as the **displacement**) over which you exert the force, times the cosine of the angle between the force and the displacement (Figure 2.1).

This is written mathematically as a "dot product" between the force vector and the distance vector.

$$W = \vec{F} \bullet \vec{d} = |F||d|\cos\theta = mad\cos\theta$$

This says that if $\vec{F}$ is parallel to $\vec{d}$ then simply $W = \vec{F} \bullet \vec{d} = |F||d|\cos(0°) = |F||d|$. But if $\vec{F}$ is perpendicular to $\vec{d}$, then $W = \vec{F} \bullet \vec{d} = |F||d|\cos(90°) = 0$. If you exert a force along the direction of motion, you do the most work. Pushing an object perpendicular to the object's motion, however, does no work at all.

This allows us an alternative definition of the joule. A joule is 1 newton-meter: one newton of force exerted over one meter of displacement. The newton has units of kg m/s². Multiplying by meters, the units of newton-meters are kg m²/s², which is the same as the units for joules, as it must be.

For almost all situations you will encounter, the angle will be one of three values: zero, 90, or 180 degrees. Most commonly, the displacement direction is the same as the force direction. For instance, if you throw a ball or lift a weight, the force and displacement are in the same direction. In this case, $\theta = 0$, so the work is simply *Fd*. One other common case is when the force is perpendicular to the direction of motion. For instance, imagine that you twirl a weight on a rope above your head. The rope is always directing a force on the weight inwards (toward your hand), but the weight is always moving tangent, along the circle. These two are at right angles, so the rope is actually doing no work on the weight. Remember, though, the rope *is* exerting a force. This is an example where the force and work differ substantially.

Rather like power, work is a quantity that is only meaningful when energy is being transferred from one form to another, or from one object to another. The work, when you calculate it this way, tells you how much energy is transferred during the process. Calculation of the quantity of work, however, does not tell you what form the energy was in before or after. Because of this, we always speak of one object doing the work and one object on which work is done.

Now we come to a subject that can be troublesome for some students. When we are calculating the "energy accounts," the amount of work done by an object must equal the amount of work done to the other. To conserve energy, the sum of the two must be zero. So, it must be the case that one is negative and the other positive, and they add up to zero (equal and opposite.) Which is positive, and which is negative?

You can look in Table 2.1 to see when work should be positive and negative. So, we should slightly modify our equation.

$$W = \pm \vec{F} \bullet \vec{d} = \pm |F||d| \cos\theta = \pm mad \cos\theta$$

You must choose the plus or minus sign correctly! This is often confusing. After we discuss the relation between work and kinetic energy, however, we will see a way to remember how to get the signs right.

TABLE 2.1 Summary of Kinetic Energy and Work Done To and By Objects

Displacement and Force on Object	Work Done on Object	Work Done by Object	Kinetic Energy of Object	Work Done by Exerter	Work Done on Exerter	Total Energy of Exerter	Example
Parallel	+	−	Increases	+	−	Decreases	Lifting a weight
Anti-parallel	−	+	Decreases	−	+	Increases	Lowering a weight
Perpen-dicular	0	0	Constant	0	0	Constant	Going in circles

WORK AND KINETIC ENERGY

How is work related to kinetic energy? Remember when you were learning to ride a bike? Your mom or dad would push you and then let go and you would coast for a while. How can you predict your final coasting speed?

Let us say they pushed you so that you accelerated at 10 m/s² over a distance of 2 m, and your mass was 25 kg. Then the force is

$$F = 25kg \times 10\frac{m}{s^2} = 250N$$

And now we can calculate the work:

$$W = Fd\cos\theta = 250N \times 2m \times (+1) = 500J$$

You accelerate in a straight line along the course, so the force was in the same direction as the displacement. The angle θ is 0, so cosθ = 1. The total work was 500 J.

PHYSICS IN HISTORY: Isaac Newton's Secret Service

As you may know, Isaac Newton is the man primarily responsible for organizing the concepts of physics with energy, force, and work. For this, he is justly revered as one of the great scientists of history. What you probably don't know is that science was not Newton's primary occupation. In fact, Isaac Newton was employed by King William III of England to detect and prosecute counterfeiters. This is what the United States Secret Service does as its primary task, in addition to protecting the president.

You have surely noticed that dimes and quarters have rifled edges. This idea is sometimes attributed to Isaac Newton. In his times (the late seventeenth century), coins were made of precious metals such as silver. Counterfeiters would remove a little bit of the edges of many coins, and thereby obtain a little bit of silver. However, removing the edges like this always leaves the edges perfectly smooth. By making the edges rifled to start with, counterfeiters could not remove the silver for themselves without being detected.

During the late seventeenth century, counterfeiting was a capital crime. Newton was responsible for the hanging of more than 100 counterfeiters. During his job at the Royal Mint, however, the physicist Daniel Bernoulli issued a challenge to all European scientists to solve two problems that had long been unsolved. Newton solved them in one evening and submitted the solution anonymously to Bernoulli. Bernoulli instantly knew who had written the solutions, saying, "I can recognize the lion by his paw."

What is the speed? Well, all this work must have gone somewhere, by conservation of energy, so where did it go? It went into increasing your kinetic energy. At the start line, the kinetic energy was

$$\frac{1}{2}mv^2 = 12.5kg \times \left(0\frac{m}{s}\right)^2 = 0J$$

Afterwards, your kinetic energy increased by 500 J:

$$KE_{final} = KE_{initial} + 500J = 0J + 500J = 500J$$

We know that the kinetic energy is 1/2 mv^2, so we can calculate v:

$$\frac{1}{2}mv^2 = 500J$$
$$v^2 = \frac{2 \times 500J}{25kg} = 40\frac{m^2}{s^2}$$
$$v = 6.3\frac{m}{s}$$

Notice what we have done. Knowing just the energy expended, we can calculate a velocity. You may have learned constant acceleration formulas such as $d = 1/2\ at^2$ in your class, but it wasn't needed. Sometimes, it is easier to use an energy-based approach to problems, and sometimes it is easier to use the time-and-force approach.

The signs involved in work can be a little bit complicated. Table 2.1 shows the signs of work and the kinetic energy. Finally, remember that work is not a form of energy. Work signifies the transfer of energy from one object to another and allows us to calculate how much energy is transferred. If we are dealing with a group or "system" of several objects, we need to take note of which object is doing what work on each other object.

MEASURING KINETIC ENERGY

How would we measure the kinetic energy of an object that we are observing? First, by examining our formula for kinetic energy:

$$KE = \frac{1}{2}mv^2$$

We need to know the object's mass and its velocity. In general, kinetic energy is not measured directly but instead mass and velocity are measured and the kinetic energy calculated. For large objects, we can generally do this in fairly obvious ways. We can use a scale to measure the mass of an object. (Most scales actually measure weight, rather than mass. An exception is a balance, which measures mass fairly directly.) There are numerous ways to measure velocity. The most direct method is simply to measure the amount of time it takes to go a certain distance. As you probably know, there are other ways—for instance, the radar gun used by police to catch highway speeders.

These, however, are not suitable ways to measure the kinetic energy of very small objects. For instance, in biology experiments, it is often necessary to measure the kinetic energy of one protein molecule or of a fragment of a single DNA strand from one cell. These microscopic objects cannot be put on a scale, nor can you easily use a stopwatch to time them. They also do not move in a straight line for very long.

Without going into great detail, it is possible to measure the kinetic energy of such tiny objects. Kinetic energies measured in such experiments are often measured in picojoules. These experiments often use special fluorescent materials to measure the time it takes to cross a certain distance and use combinations of electric and magnetic fields to measure the mass.

KINETIC ENERGY AND COLLISIONS

When two moving objects collide, conservation of kinetic energy leads us to be able to make conclusions about what could possibly happen as a result of the collision. If you throw a bowling ball down the alley at the pins, the pins fly off very fast, but not infinitely fast. How fast they could go is already limited by the amount of kinetic energy transferred to the pins by the bowling ball. For instance, imagine we have a collision between two objects. One has mass m_1 and velocity v_1; the other has mass m_2 and velocity v_2. Then the total kinetic energy in the collision is

$$\frac{1}{2}m_1 v_1^2 + \frac{1}{2}m_2 v_2^2$$

What is the largest possible velocity v_{1m} for object 1? Suppose after the collision, object 2 stops and object 1 carries all the kinetic energy. Then

$$KE = \frac{1}{2}m_1v_1^2 + \frac{1}{2}m_2v_2^2$$

$$\frac{1}{2}m_1v_{1m}^2 + \frac{1}{2}m_2\left(0\right)^2 = \frac{1}{2}m_1v_1^2 + \frac{1}{2}m_2v_2^2$$

$$\frac{1}{2}m_1v_{1m}^2 = \frac{1}{2}m_1v_1^2 + \frac{1}{2}m_2v_2^2$$

$$v_{1m} = \sqrt{\frac{m_1v_1^2 + m_2v_2^2}{m_1}}$$

You can calculate in the same way that the maximum possible velocity for object 2, if object 1 is at rest after the collision, is

$$v_{2m} = \sqrt{\frac{m_1v_1^2 + m_2v_2^2}{m_2}}$$

For instance, in a bowling alley, the bowling ball might have a mass of 5 kg and be moving at 3 m/s. The pins might have a mass of 1.5 kg; they start at rest. Then, the maximum possible velocity of a pin after a collision would be

$$v_{2m} = \sqrt{\frac{m_1v_1^2 + m_2v_2^2}{m_2}} = \sqrt{\frac{5kg \times \left(3\frac{m}{s}\right)^2 + 1.5kg \times \left(0\frac{m}{s}\right)^2}{1.5kg}} = 5.5\frac{m}{s}$$

There are other considerations in collisions, which are due to conservation of momentum. The momentum of an object is its mass times its velocity. Without going into details of momentum, we cannot say more than what the maximum possible velocities are—in particular, we cannot say what velocities actually will result. When

APPLIED PHYSICS: Roller Coasters

If you go to Cedar Point Park in Sandusky, Ohio, you will find 17 roller coasters ready for your entertainment. The tallest roller coaster is more than 400 feet tall. Another very interesting coaster there is more than 300 feet tall—that's about 100 meters. Let us walk through the energy at the various points along the ride:

1. At the beginning: The passengers have just gotten in and the roller coaster is not yet moving.
2. Moving up the slope: A winch system pulls the roller coaster 100 meters upwards. This winch does work, transferring the energy of the winch system into the potential energy of the roller coaster.
3. At the top: The roller coaster is moving very slowly just as it reaches the top of the highest climb. The roller coasters have a typical mass of 2,000 kg; at 100 meters in the air, its potential energy is 2 million joules.
4. The roller coaster rolls downhill without power. All the energy comes from the potential energy of the starting height. It speeds up as it goes downhill.
5. The roller coaster heads back uphill. It does *not* need any more power to do this. It converts some of the kinetic energy back to potential energy.
6. It heads back down again, converting fully back to kinetic energy.
7. The roller coaster continues to convert energy back and forth between kinetic and potential energy, without ever needing an additional source of power. There is no motor in the roller coaster.
8. Eventually, friction brakes turn all the kinetic and potential energy into heat energy. The brake pads become very hot, but the roller coaster comes to a halt with zero potential energy and zero kinetic energy.

Figure 2.2 *It took a lot of energy to distort the metal and rubber on this car.*

you consider momentum, it is possible to calculate precisely what the final velocities are and not just their maximum values.

One interesting thing happens in many collisions. It is not uncommon that in a car crash, both cars come to rest, even though the initial kinetic energy is often very large—millions of joules. Where does this energy go? It gets divided into many different kinds of energy. The most noticeable, at first, is the loud "crashing" noise, which does require energy to make (although it is, in fact, rather little energy). Also, the steel beams and plastic and glass of the car have been twisted and shattered (Figure 2.2). This took energy as well. And there is a lot of heat, especially where the cars contacted and where the tires contacted the ground. The heat is usually enough to burn some of the rubber on the tires.

This kind of collision, when the total kinetic energy afterward is less than before, is called an **inelastic collision**. It does not mean energy was destroyed; it only means some of it was changed from kinetic energy into another form of energy, often heat.

KINETIC ENERGY OF ROTATION

When an object is rotating, it has kinetic energy, even if it is not moving from place to place. So, it takes energy in order to set a merry-go-round spinning, even though it does not move across the park. The subject of energy of rotation is pretty complex, and we won't get into all of it here. We can, however, explore two fairly simple cases. The first case is the weight-on-a-string.

The Olympic hammer throw competition involves hurling a 7kg weight on the end of a 2m steel cable. To throw it the maximum distance, the athlete wants to impart as much energy to the ball as possible. The athletes spin themselves around, and when they feel they cannot spin any faster, they release the "hammer" to fly.

Most athletes reach a maximum rotation speed of one rotation per second. How much energy is in the hammer when spinning at this speed? In one second (the rotation period), the ball makes one complete trip around a circle that is 2 meters in radius (the length of the steel cable) and therefore $2\pi r$ meters in circumference. So we can calculate the velocity:

$$v = \frac{2\pi r}{1s} = \frac{2\pi \times 2m}{1s} = 12.6\frac{m}{s}$$

We know how to calculate the kinetic energy, since we know the velocity and mass:

$$KE = \frac{1}{2}mv^2 = 552J$$

So, if a weight on a string swings through one circle of radius r in a **period of time** T and has radius r and mass m, then the kinetic energy of rotation is

$$KE = \frac{1}{2}m\left(\frac{2\pi r}{T}\right)^2$$

Now let us think about a bicycle wheel. It has many light spokes and most of the weight is in the rim and tire. Imagine you chopped up the wheel (Figure 2.3). Then, each piece of the wheel-and-spoke would be like the weight-and-cable we calculated. The first piece would have mass m_1 and kinetic energy

$$KE = \frac{1}{2}m_1\left(\frac{2\pi r}{T}\right)^2$$

And we would add up all the little pieces:

$$KE = \frac{1}{2}m_1\left(\frac{2\pi r}{T}\right)^2 + \frac{1}{2}m_2\left(\frac{2\pi r}{T}\right)^2 + \frac{1}{2}m_3\left(\frac{2\pi r}{T}\right)^2 + ...$$

$$= \frac{1}{2}(m_1 + m_2 + m_3 + ...)\left(\frac{2\pi r}{T}\right)^2$$

But if you add up all the little masses $(m_1 + m_2 + m_3 + ...)$, then that is just the original bicycle wheel mass m. So the formula

$$KE = \frac{1}{2}m\left(\frac{2\pi r}{T}\right)^2$$

also works when the mass is not a ball rotating on a string, but is a spinning hoop with spokes.

This formula, however, does not work for all shapes. A spinning sphere (for instance, if you take a globe and spin it around) has a slightly different formula, and a spinning disk also has a different formula for the energy it requires. Luckily, the most common things that spin are wheels, and they generally follow this formula.

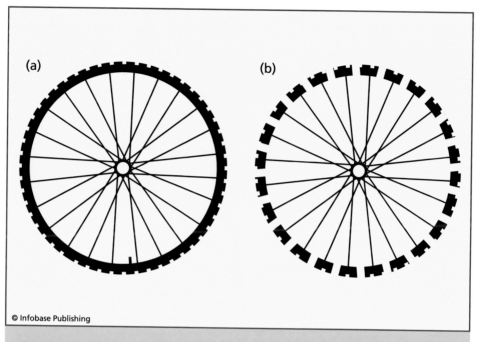

Figure 2.3 *(a) A bicycle wheel and its spokes. (b) The bicycle wheel chopped into small pieces. The total of the small pieces is the same as the whole wheel, but now each individual piece acts like a weight on a string.*

SKATERS, BIKES, AND HAMMERS

A very fast skater might reach speeds of 15 m/s (about 35 miles per hour). If the skater weighs 45 kg, we can find their energy of motion:

$$KE = \frac{1}{2}mv^2 = \frac{1}{2}45kg \times \left(15\frac{m}{s}\right)^2 = 5062J$$

In the chapter title, we rounded this to 5,000 joules. So that we can have some understanding of how much energy this is, this amount of energy is approximately the same as:

- a biker going 35 miles per hour
- a 1,000kg car going 7 miles per hour

- a bowling ball going 100 miles per hour
- a bowling pin going 200 miles per hour
- an Olympic hammer rotating 3 times per second
- a 2kg bicycle wheel spinning 10 times every second.

CHAPTER 3

Potential Energy of Liberty's Torch: 3.4 Million Joules

WHAT HAPPENS WHEN YOU DROP YOUR PENCIL? EASY—IT falls down, gaining speed, until it hits the ground. Just before it hits the ground, you could measure its speed—it is certainly not zero! Its mass is not zero, either, so its kinetic energy is also not zero.

This situation, just before it hits the ground, is one in which we can calculate the total amount of energy, using $KE = 1/2mv^2$. This is very puzzling, because before you dropped your pencil, it was not moving. Therefore, its kinetic energy was zero before you dropped it. We might suspect that before it was dropped the pencil had another form of energy that was somehow transformed into kinetic energy as the pencil fell. We must learn how to calculate, and the calculation of this new energy has something to do with the position of the pencil just before it fell.

In fact, this energy, known as **potential energy**, is probably the most common form of energy in the world. We can define it a little more precisely in a moment, but let us just get some intuitive idea what it might be. Potential energy is essentially the energy that an object has "stored up," due to having had work done on it in the past.

Let us go back to our pencil. Suppose earlier in the day, it had fallen to the floor. You picked it up, and set it on your desk. Later in the day, it fell back to the floor. What has happened, energetically speaking, to the pencil in this cycle?

First, you picked it up. You exerted a force on the pencil as you brought it upwards. The force that you exerted was mg—the mass m of the pencil times the acceleration g of gravity—in order to just barely overcome gravity and slowly move it upwards at a constant speed. What work did you do on it? You did $Fd\cos\theta$. If your desk is at a height h, the amount of work done was mgh.

Now, the pencil is on your desk, not moving, but you have done work on it. This work must have been converted into some sort of energy. And in fact the amount of energy that was done is mgh. It's not kinetic energy, it's not heat, and it's not electrical. But you know that if you drop the pencil, it will gain kinetic energy as it falls (since it will speed up until it hits the ground). So, even though this energy is not obviously visible as the pencil sits on your desk, it is real. It came from the work your muscles did as you lifted it. The energy of lifting is now "stored" in the object. This kind of unobvious energy that comes from work done in the past is called potential energy.

This is a little bit mysterious, so let us probe it a little more. Where is this energy stored? To answer that, first let's recognize why we had to do work in the first place: because there was a gravitational field caused by the enormous mass of the Earth. When we lifted the pencil, we changed the distance between the pencil and the center of the Earth—we changed the position of the pencil in the Earth's gravitational field. For this reason, we would call the potential energy **gravitational potential energy**. The energy is due to the configuration of pencil and gravitational field. If we return to the old configuration (pencil on the floor), we must recover the work that was done in the first place (i.e., in the form of kinetic energy).

In all cases of potential energy, you will find that the work that was done was due to the influence of some field of force. In doing the work, the configuration of objects in the field was changed. This new and different configuration is why a potential for energy exists. For instance, by returning to the original configuration, the work that was done can be released—often as kinetic energy. It can also be released in other ways, for instance, as heat.

The field need not always be gravitational. In fact, most usable potential energy in the world is due to the configuration of electrical charges in an electric field. You do not need to know all the details of electric fields to understand this. Just as in the case of gravity, electric fields exert forces on charges. If you do work to move charges in the fields and change the configuration, the charge will come to have potential energy. In this case, it will be **electrical potential** energy.

Is potential energy really energy? Or is it just an accounting trick to make it seem that energy is conserved? In short, potential energy is real energy. Compare potential energy to kinetic energy. We can calculate how much kinetic energy there is. It can be transferred to other forms of energy (like heat), or to other objects. It comes about as a result of work done, a force times a displacement. And it forms part of a system total energy that must be conserved. Potential energy shares every one of these properties, just like kinetic energy.

KINETICS, POTENTIAL, AND BALLISTICS

Early studies of kinetic and potential energies actually came from the work of Benjamin Robins, who put Isaac Newton's theories to the test in order to improve the English army's understanding of **ballistics**. Ballistics is the study of the path of projectiles after they have been launched (Figure 3.1). The English army was interested in how to improve the accuracy of their artillery weapons.

When a projectile is launched straight upwards, its basic path can be described as:

- starting with an initial upwards velocity v_0
- rising, and simultaneously slowing down

Figure 3.1 *When a projectile is launched upwards, its energy passes from kinetic, to potential, and back to kinetic.*

- reaching the top of its flight, where for an instant the velocity is 0
- falling, and speeding up (downwards)
- returning to the ground at a high final velocity.

We might wonder what the final velocity of the projectile must be when it returns to the ground. If there is no friction due to air resistance, we can use energy conservation to figure this out. Because the total energy of the projectile is conserved, when the projectile returns to its starting point, the kinetic energy must be the same as when it left the cannon. So, the final velocity speed must be equal to the initial speed; except that the velocity vector has changed direction from upwards to downwards.

Again, if there is no friction, what height must the projectile reach? The total energy, kinetic plus potential, as it is launched, is

$$KE + PE = \frac{1}{2}mv_0^2 + mgh = \frac{1}{2}mv_0^2 + mg \times 0 = \frac{1}{2}mv_0^2$$

When it reaches the top, the velocity (for an instant) is 0, so the total energy is

$$KE + PE = \frac{1}{2}mv^2 + mgh = \frac{1}{2}m(0)^2 + mgh = mgh$$

Because energy is conserved, these two must be equal, so

$$h = \frac{v_0^2}{2g}$$

So, knowing the initial velocity, we can calculate the height that the projectile reaches. When it reaches that height, the kinetic energy has been changed entirely to potential energy. When it reaches the ground again, it's like dropping the projectile from that height: the potential energy changes back into kinetic energy. So, the process of rising and falling, when written in terms of energy, looks like this:

- Initially all of the projectile's energy is kinetic.
- As the projectile rises, its kinetic energy is being converted into potential energy (slowing down, but rising in height).
- At the top, all the energy is potential (no velocity, only height).
- As the projectile falls, potential energy is being converted back to kinetic (lowering in height, and speeding up).
- Finally, when the projectile nears the ground all of its energy is kinetic (the change in potential is 0).

Of course, an English cannoneer who fired straight up would not be of much use to the army! Instead, it is even more useful to determine the maximum range of a projectile, if it is fired at an angle. Benjamin Robins determined that if there is no air resistance, a cannonball fired at a 45° angle sails the farthest. Its maximum distance d_{max} is related to the initial kinetic energy KE, the mass of the projectile m, and the acceleration of gravity g:

$$d_{max} = \frac{2 \times KE}{mg}$$

Mr. Robins also determined that when you consider air resistance, the maximum range angle is actually closer to 30 degrees and the maximum range is reduced. But the essence of the situation is the same: The higher the initial energy, the farther the projectile will go.

THE ZERO-POINT OF POTENTIAL ENERGY

The measurement of potential energy mgh is always a little indirect. Why? The potential energy depends on how you measure h. Suppose your pencil is on your desk in a classroom on the fourth floor of your school. Or perhaps the pencil is on a desk on the first floor or in the basement. Is the potential energy of the pencil on the desk the same in each case? If you choose to measure the height h of the pencil from the floor to the desktop, the pencil's potential energy mgh is the same whether the desk is on the first floor, fourth floor, or the basement. If you choose to measure the height h of the pencil from the ground level to the desktop, the pencils on the different floors have different potential energies (Figure 3.2).

Nevertheless, when you push the pencil off the desktop, it falls to the floor, no matter if the desk is on the fourth floor, first floor, or basement floor. The potential energy difference between (a) the pencil on the desk and (b) the pencil on the floor is what causes the motion of the pencil. This potential energy difference is the same regardless of whether the floor is below the Earth's ground, above ground, or at ground level. The potential energy difference, however, between (a) the pencil on the desk and (b) the pencil on

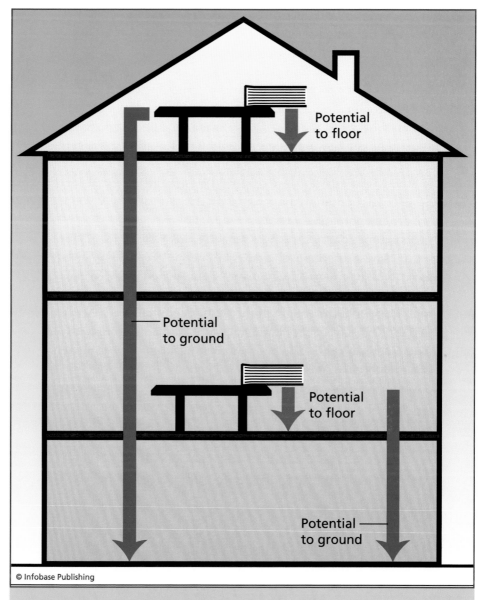

Potential
to floor

Potential
to ground

Potential
to floor

Potential
to ground

Figure 3.2 *The potential difference from desk to floor is the same no matter where in the school you are. The potential difference to the ground level, however, is different for each floor.*

the (Earth's) ground does of course depend on where the desk is in relation to the ground.

This brings us to recognize that only potential energy *differences* are meaningful. You can define two configurations (i.e., one configuration is the pencil on the desk, another configuration is the pencil falling to the floor) and ask what is the potential energy difference between them—that is a meaningful question, and the answer tells you how much energy will be released (or, if negative, how much must be put in) when going from one configuration to the other. So to answer the question "What is the potential energy of this configuration?" you have to define carefully how you will measure the potential energy.

Sometimes physics teachers rephrase this fact, saying, "We are free to choose the zero of potential energy." Probably you have used a scale, perhaps in chemistry class, which allowed you to "zero" the scale with a container on top of it. You could have simply measured the weight of the container and object, then subtracted the weight of the container. But it was easier simply to put the container on the scale and zero it. The idea is the same with potential energy. You can take the difference in potential energy between two configurations, or you could define one configuration as having zero potential energy. In either case, you are really taking the difference, just as on the scale all you are really doing is subtracting the weight of the container.

So, now we can correct our earlier statement that the potential energy of the pencil is *mgh*. In fact, we should have said that the potential energy *change* in lifting the pencil to your desk was $mg\Delta h$.

WORK, POTENTIAL, KINETIC, AND LIFTING

If you want to know for sure that you are really doing work, recognize that work can always be used, one way or another, to move a mass. In fact, it is useful to draw little diagrams to convince yourself that you are dealing with work rather than, for instance, heat.

Potential and kinetic energy are sometimes collectively called mechanical energy. Potential and kinetic energy are always fully

TABLE 3.1	**Summary of Mechanical Energy and Work Done To and By Objects**						
Displace-ment & Force on Object	**Work Done on Object**	**Work Done by Object**	**Mechanical Energy Change of Object**	**Work Done by Exerter**	**Work Done on Exerter**	**Mechanical Energy Change of Exerter**	**Example**
Parallel	+	–	Increases (+)	+	–	Decreases (–)	Lifting a weight
Anti-parallel	–	+	Decreases (–)	–	+	Increases (+)	Lower-ing a weight
Perpen-dicular	0	0	Constant	0	0	Constant	Going in circles

available to be converted into work and into each other. Table 3.1, very similar to the table in the previous chapter, is now updated to include potential energy. So, mechanical energy can be any com-bination of potential and kinetic energy.

Table 3.1 also brings an interesting point to our attention. For any object (or exerter), the change in mechanical energy (E_M) has a sign opposite to the work done by the object and equal to work done on the object. So, we have the following relations:

$$\Delta E_M = -W_{by}$$
$$\Delta E_M = W_{to}$$

Again, the ΔE_M can be purely potential energy changes, purely kinetic energy changes, or a combination of the two.

For instance, Figure 3.3 shows (a) an example of using kinetic energy to do work in lifting a weight and (b) an example of using gravitational potential energy to do work in lifting a weight. In

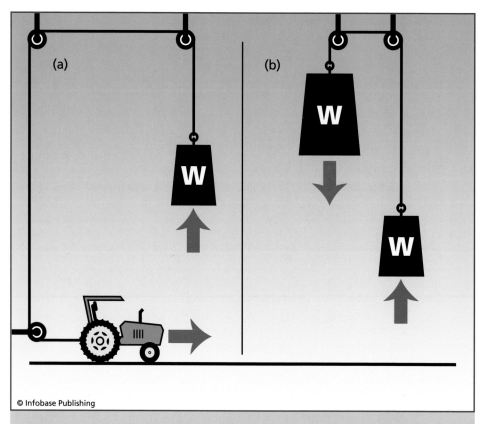

Figure 3.3 *(a) Using kinetic energy to lift a weight. (b) Using gravitational potential energy to lift a weight. In general, if you can figure out a way to lift a weight, then the situation has the possibility to do work.*

general, if you can use the situation to lift a weight (and thereby do real work), the situation is suitable for extracting work.

ESCAPE VELOCITY

The Earth orbits the Sun, year after year, without flying away from it. We say that the Earth is gravitationally bound to the Sun. What does this mean? It means that if you want to pull the Earth very far away from the Sun (that is, so that it could escape from the Sun), you would have to add energy.

Let us imagine the Earth was in fact pulled far away from the Sun—all the way almost to infinite distance—and then left at rest. The Earth would start at rest, but feel a very weak, distant tug from the Sun's gravity. The Earth would slowly accelerate toward the Sun, and the gravitational pull of the Sun would increase. The Earth would be pulled more and more toward the Sun, gaining speed as it did so.

In this case, the Earth is gaining kinetic energy as it moves closer. This means that it loses potential energy as it gets closer to the Sun. The moving Earth behaves exactly the same as your falling pencil did! The falling pencil loses potential energy as it moves downwards toward the floor. Whenever an object moves in the direction of the force, it loses potential energy and gains kinetic energy; we say the forces do positive work on the object. When the object moves against the direction of the force, we say that the force is doing negative work, and the potential energy increases by the amount of work done.

Thus, if the Earth were to escape the Sun, we would have to add work to move the Earth to the higher potential energy further from the Sun. The positive work that it would take to completely separate the Earth and Sun produces a potential energy, called the **binding energy**. In this case, the binding energy is gravitational. We will see in the course of this book, however, that there can be other forms of binding energy.

ACTIVATION ENERGY

Everyone knows that water runs downhill. How is it then that there can be lakes in the mountains? Why doesn't all the water run out of the lake and down to lower potential energy? (Figure 3.4)

The reason is that to flow downhill, the water would first have to climb up the banks of the lake or over a dam before flowing down the other side. Temporarily, the water would have to move to a higher potential energy, but the total net effect in the end would be to reach a lower potential energy. This would release the water's potential energy of being in the mountain heights. This energy might be released as kinetic energy (the water rushing downhill faster and faster) or it might be released

You Can't Always Escape

Usually, when you throw something upward, its maximum height is reached when the potential energy mgh equals the initial kinetic energy $1/2mv^2$:

$$h = \frac{v^2}{2g}$$

This formula assumes, however, that the projectile doesn't go up very far, so that gravity is constant. When the projectile goes very high, gravity (g) is less as you get further from the Earth. And because g is less, the projectile actually goes higher than you would calculate from this formula.

You might imagine that if you threw it hard enough, it would just keep going and going and would never fall back to the Earth. For every gravitational field, there is some such velocity, called the **escape velocity**—if you throw or fire or launch something with velocity greater than the escape velocity, it will keep on going and never fall back to Earth. In this case, the kinetic energy you give to the projectile is larger than the binding energy of the object to the Earth.

In the table are the escape velocities for several gravitation fields: for escaping the Earth, for escaping the Sun (launching from the Earth), for escaping the Moon, and escaping Saturn, and so on.

One other thing you might want to escape the gravity of, if you came near it, is the gravity of the massive black hole at the center of our galaxy. Its escape velocity is 5.4×10^8 m/s. You might notice a problem with this speed—it is greater than the speed of light. Since nothing can move as heat (the rushing water rubbing against the rocks on the way down, heating both rocks and water due to friction), or a human construction might be able to turn the potential energy release into electrical energy.

faster than light, you can never have enough energy to escape a black hole. Neither can any light escape, which is why a black hole is black. Once you are in a black hole, you can never escape.

TABLE 3.2 Escape Velocities for Several Gravitation Fields

ESCAPING THE PULL OF:	FROM:	VELOCITY (KM/S)	VELOCITY (MILES/S)
Moon	Moon's surface	2	1.2
Earth	Earth's surface	11	6.8
Jupiter	Jupiter's surface	60	37
Saturn	Saturn's surface	36	22
Sun	Earth's surface	42	26
Sun	Sun's surface	618	386
Milky Way galaxy	Earth's surface	1,000	625

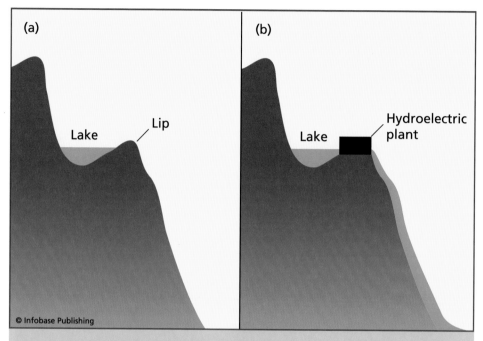

Figure 3.4 *Cross-section of lake geography: (a) A lip prevents the water from flowing downhill. (b) Using the potential energy of a high mountain lake to generate hydro-electric power.*

This little bit of energy needed to get the release started is called the **activation energy**. The activation energy is regained as released energy as soon as the water falls down the other side of the mountain to the same height as the original lake. The net energy release is the difference between the lake height and the bottom of the mountain. Activation energies occur in many everyday instances. For example, a piece of paper can burn and release energy, but to start the process, activation energy must be added to it, in the form of a hot match.

The story of the mountain lake should remind you always that the "zero" point of potential energy can be assigned anywhere.

Maybe the "bottom of the mountain" is just another lake, still high above sea level.

LADY LIBERTY'S TORCH

The Statue of Liberty was raised in New York City in 1884, a gift from the people of France to the people of the United States. It was shipped from France by boat in 350 pieces in 214 crates. The final piece to go into place was Lady Liberty's torch, which at its tip is 93 meters above the ground. (The statue is 46 meters tall; the pedestal on which it stands is 47 meters tall.) Each fingernail weighs 2 kg.

The torch has actually been rebuilt several times. It consists of a "flame" portion, internal steel ribs, a steel walkway, and copper sheeting. Originally, the torch was of copper, as the rest of the statue. In 1916, the flame was redesigned, made of 600 yellow-glass plates. In 1984, it was redesigned again, made of gold plating over copper sheeting; and the new torch was then lifted back onto the statue (Figure 3.5).

Though the entire torch has never been weighed on a scale, it is estimated to have a mass of 3,700 kg (a little more than 4 tons.) Using what we know now about potential energy, what is its potential energy at its height of 93 meters compared to when it was on the ground? (Note that this is the same as the work required to lift the torch up to its position.) The potential energy difference is

$$\Delta PE = mgh = 3700 kg \times 9.8 \frac{m}{s^2} \times 93m = 3.4 MJ$$

To get an idea just how much energy 3.4 million joules is, it is the same as:

- a 1,000 kg car going 185 miles per hour
- eight 1,000 kg cars going 65 miles per hour
- a 12-pound (5.4 kg) cannonball shot to a height of 63 km
- 80 minutes of continuous power output by a strong horse

Figure 3.5 *After being redesigned and rebuilt, it took a lot of energy to lift the Statue of Liberty's torch back onto the statue.*

- a water balloon falling from a height of 500 km
- a golf ball launched with enough velocity to escape the Earth's gravitation.

So, we could use the energy of the Statue of Liberty's torch to send a golf ball to the stars!

CHAPTER 4

Heat Power of the Sun in 1 m²: 1,500 Watts

HEAT IS OBVIOUSLY RELATED TO ENERGY. THE SUN'S ENERGY heats the Earth. We use the energy in heating oil to warm our homes in the winter. We use energy in burning logs to heat a fireplace, and the electricity that gives us light from a light bulb also causes the light bulb to heat up.

Heat, however, is not the only thing we need to understand here. We also know heat is related to temperature somehow, so we need to look at **thermal energy**, which you may not have heard of. (The most common everyday use of the term is in geothermal energy, such as using the heat of underground hot springs as an energy source.)

What happens when an object heats up (that is, when its temperature increases)? The **temperature** of an object reflects how much the molecules of the object are randomly jittering around (Figure 4.1). The temperature reflects the average kinetic energy of the molecules—if they are moving around, they have kinetic

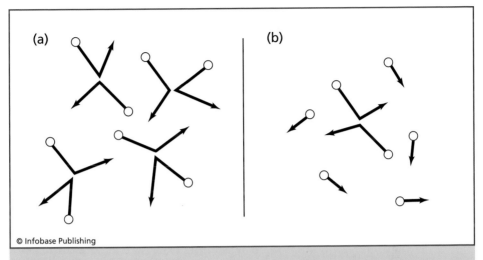

© Infobase Publishing

Figure 4.1 *Random motions in a gas due to thermal energy. (a) At high temperatures, there are many collisions and the molecules move at a very high speed (high kinetic energy.) (b) At lower temperatures, the molecules move more slowly and collide more rarely.*

energy. The faster they are jittering, the higher the kinetic energy, since $KE = 1/2\ mv^2$.

In a solid object, the molecules are all more or less "in place" as they jitter. They are arranged in a regular structure and each molecule moves back and forth around its place in the structure. In a liquid, the molecules are not ordered. The molecules move about, bumping up against other molecules, jittering as they slowly travel from one place to another. Because the molecules are so tightly packed together, they bounce back and forth off of one another, only slowly making any progress in one direction or another.

In a gas, the molecules are much freer to zoom about at high speed, going a fair distance before they bounce up against another molecule. In an ideal gas made of single atoms, one can define the relation between the temperature T of the gas and kinetic energy of one single atom in the gas:

$$KE = \frac{3}{2} k_B T$$

The constant k_B is called **Boltzmann's constant**, and has a value of 1.4×10^{-23} J/K. *The thermal energy of the gas is the sum total of all the kinetic energies of all the molecules in the gas.* It obviously depends on the temperature and on the number of atoms in the gas. The total thermal energy is $n_{atom} \times 3/2 \, k_B T$.

Staring at this formula for a moment, those of you from northern climes may notice something horribly amiss. What if the temperature is below zero? Kinetic energy can never be negative! You are correct to notice this, and it brings us to the question of temperature scale. You are likely familiar with Celsius and Fahrenheit as two different ways of measuring temperature. We need a third scale, one that is never negative.

This scale, known as the **Kelvin** scale, uses units that are the same size as the Celsius scale. That is, a change of 1 degree kelvin (K) is the same as 1 degree Celsius. (Remember, 1 degree Fahrenheit change is only 5/9 of the temperature change of 1 degree Celsius.) To convert from degrees Celsius to kelvins, take the Celsius temperature and add 273 degrees (Table 4.1).

It turns out that for normal objects, no temperature can ever be below 0 kelvin (–273 Celsius). How can we imagine 0 kelvin?

TABLE 4.1	Correspondence Among Kelvin, Celsius, and Fahrenheit Scales	
KELVIN	**CELSIUS**	**FAHRENHEIT**
373	100	212
273	0 (Freezing)	32
0	–273	–460

If temperature is related to kinetic energy, then when the random jittering kinetic energy of molecules is 0, the temperature should be 0. It is not that hard to imagine an object where all the molecules are perfectly still and in place; this object would have a temperature of exactly 0 (often called "absolute zero").

So, temperature essentially measures the average random jittering kinetic energy of individual molecules, and thermal energy is the total amount of random kinetic jittering energy by all the molecules in the object.

HEAT

What, then, is heat? Unfortunately, the concept of heat is often used a bit imprecisely in science textbooks and in scientific discussions. Most precisely, heat is the transfer of thermal energy to or from an object. In this way, it is like work—it only refers to the amount transferred. It is generally positive if the energy is transferred to an object and negative if transferred out of an object.

You should be aware, however, that *heat* is often used to refer to thermal energy. This use is technically incorrect but common enough that you should be aware of it. In fact, this use is enshrined in textbook chemistry terms, such as "latent heat." One reason this can be confusing is that when heat is transferred, the thermal energy of some object in the transfer must be changing—otherwise we'd simply call it work. The other object in the transfer, however, might not change its thermal energy by the same amount. Instead, it may convert some of the transferred thermal energy into another form, such as potential energy or kinetic energy.

Thus, heat is like work—a transfer of energy, and it is positive or negative. Why not just call it work? There is an important reason that we keep heat separate from work. Thermal energy, because it results from random motion, is special in some ways. In particular, it turns out not to be possible to convert thermal energy perfectly into kinetic or potential energy. (There is no such restriction on potential or kinetic energy—they can be perfectly converted into one another, or completely into heat.) When heat is transferred, some of it must always remain unconverted as thermal energy.

This is actually a restatement of the second law of **thermodynamics**. You may have heard of this law as saying, "The randomness in the universe always increases." Just as there are many equivalent ways of calculating the motion of an object (by energy or forces), there are several equivalent ways to state the second law. Another restatement is that "heat never flows spontaneously from cold to hot."

Mechanical energy usually involves a force or motion pointing in one direction. For instance, the force you are trying to exert in order to do work needs to be in one particular direction. So mechanical energy has special direction or order to it. But heat is due to the random jiggling of many molecules. It is possible to straighten many of them out, but you can never stop all of them jiggling, because that would become much less random, and the second law requires the randomness to increase.

In fact, the second law dictates exactly how much of the heat may be converted into other forms of energy and how much must remain as thermal energy. If the heat is flowing from an object with temperature T_H to an object with temperature T_L, the maximum allowed fraction of the heat that can be converted to other forms of energy besides thermal energy is:

$$f_{max} = 1 - \frac{T_L}{T_H}$$

This is called the **Carnot limit**. You have to express the temperature in kelvins to calculate the maximum fraction that can be converted for T_H and T_L. Because both T_L and T_H are positive (or at least not negative), and T_H is not zero, f_{max} is always a number between one (if T_H is infinity) and zero (if T_L equals T_H). If T_H is any value of temperature besides infinity, the maximum efficiency is less than 100%.

This formula, due to the second law of thermodynamics, has profound implications for extracting useful work (potential or kinetic energy) from heat. If we wish to use thermal energy to perform work, we need the temperature of the initial object with thermal energy to be as high as possible and the temperature of the final object as low as possible.

This is why engines are so hot! They extract thermal energy from gasoline—to convert it most efficiently to kinetic energy (velocity of the car), it needs to be at a high temperature. The low temperature is provided by cooling other parts of the engine by circulating coolant through the radiator, which allows the heat to escape to the atmosphere (the air as it passes through the radiator).

HEAT TRANSFER: CONDUCTION, CONVECTION, AND RADIATION

As you know, heat is transferred from hotter things to colder things. This is evident every time you touch something colder than yourself (you feel heat leaving you, which gives the sensation of being cool) or touch something warmer than yourself (you feel heat entering you, giving you the sensation of warmth). How does this happen? There are three ways that heat can move from one place to another: conduction, convection, and radiation.

Conduction is the most basic form of heat transfer. Heat is transferred when two bodies (of different temperatures) are in direct contact. Remember that the thermal energy of an object is the random motion of its molecules. When the objects are in direct contact, the molecules of one bump directly into the molecules of the other. This transfers kinetic energy from the hotter object (whose molecules slow down during the collisions) to the colder object (whose molecules speed up during the collisions). Conduction also occurs between objects and gases. A very hot oven can heat the air in a kitchen by conduction. And the air, in turn, can heat you by conduction, even though you are not in direct contact with the oven providing the original heat.

Much of heat transfer over any distance occurs through **convection**. In conduction, heat moves from one place to another because molecules collide with their neighbors. Because molecules are very small, this transfers heat over small distances. Eventually, as neighbors pass heat to neighbors to the next neighbors, the heat can travel some distance; but this takes a very long time. Rapid heat transfer usually takes place by simply moving the hot object itself.

This is how most heating or cooling systems work. For instance, the cooling system in a car uses water to remove heat from the engine. Most of the heat is removed simply by having the water, which is hot, move from one place to another. Other examples of convection are in the atmosphere (where hot air moves upward due to its low density), ocean (where cold waters in the North Atlantic sink to the bottom), and room fans (which move cool air from one part of a room to another). In each case, the object (water or air) with the desired temperature is moved rather than letting the heat conduct.

Finally, heat can be transferred by **radiation**. Here, we do not mean the kind of radiation associated with nuclear physics. Instead, we mean the word related to "radiate"—light. Heat can be transferred from one place to another by light instead of by convection or conduction. The hot object that emits the light reduces its thermal energy because it has released the light—therefore, it cools off. The object that later absorbs this light will warm up because it has gained new energy from this light.

HEAT, LIGHT, AND THE SUN

It comes as no surprise to learn that hot objects often give off light. The most commonplace examples of this are charcoal and incandescent lightbulbs. Charcoal in a barbecue, once it has heated up, begins to glow an orange-red color. The center of a briquette of charcoal can reach more than 1,000° Celsius, though the outer surface is often somewhat cooler. Similarly, an incandescent filament, which gives off the light in a lightbulb, can reach temperatures of 2,000° Celsius!

Hot objects give off light, but what color of light they give off will depend on the temperature. **Light** is a special kind of wave. Waves have "**wavelengths**": When you throw a rock into a pond, you can see the ripples are spaced less than a meter apart. Ocean waves, however, are often spaced more than a hundred meters apart. The distance between the waves is called the wavelength. Light is not a water wave, but it also has wavelengths—different colors of light have different wavelengths.

When an object is heated to a certain wavelength, it gives out light predominantly of one wavelength—that is, of a particular color. What color it is depends on the temperature of the object. Relatively lower temperature objects (say, around 1,500°C) will glow more red; somewhat higher temperature objects (around 2,500°C) will glow more yellow; yet hotter objects (5,000°C) will have more of a blue-white glow. You are probably used to thinking of blue as colder and red as hotter, but when it comes to light emission from hot objects, it is in fact the opposite.

Because different colors of light simply have different wave-lengths, the range of possible light "colors" ranges from wavelengths of 0 meters to wavelengths of infinite length (Figure 4.2). Light, however, is only visible to our eyes when its wavelength is between 400 and 800 nanometers (nm)—about one-millionth of a meter or one-thousandth of a millimeter.

Light of longer wavelengths has several ranges: from **infrared** light (between roughly 800 and 100,000 nanometers), to **microwaves** (roughly 100 micrometers to 10 centimeters), to radio waves (roughly 10 centimeters to 10 meters). Yes, microwaves in a microwave oven are a form of light, and radio waves you hear with a radio are also forms of light, but they are forms of light that are not visible to the human eye.

Light of shorter wavelengths also has several ranges. From roughly 400 nm down to 10 nm, the light is called **ultraviolet** (UV) light. From 10 nm to about 10-trillionths of a meter, the light is called **X-rays**. And light with wavelengths below 10-trillionths of a meter is generally referred to as **gamma rays**. Again, you should notice that something you thought of as separate and special— X-rays—is really a form of light with a different wavelength.

Finally, let us go back to an earlier statement and refine it. "When an object is heated to a certain wavelength, it gives out light predominantly of one wavelength—that is, of a particular

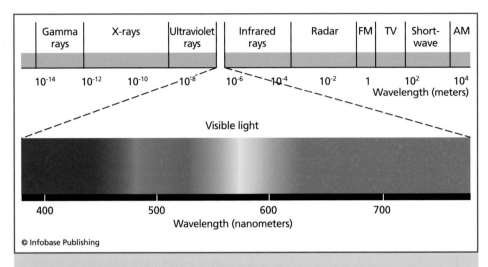

Figure 4.2 *The spectrum of light, visible and invisible, showing the relation between type (or color) and wavelength.*

color." In fact, a hot object emits light of many different wavelengths, with most of the wavelengths near the predominant one. This is the same way that basketball teams have predominantly tall players, but not all of them are exactly the same height.

This is familiar from, most simply, fire. The "thing" that is hot in this case is actually tiny grains of soot. Just as charcoal in a barbecue glows as it gets hot, the tiny soot grains grow hot and glow in the flame. There are so many tiny grains spread through the air that the air itself appears to be glowing.

In fact, for most of the objects and temperatures we meet every day, most of the light produced is infrared light. Most objects around us are always glowing due just to their thermal energy, but they are glowing in a "color" (wavelength) humans cannot see. Many mechanical devices, however, such as night-vision goggles, can see this kind of light. These devices allow the user to "see" hot

Infrared Vision

*O*bjects with temperatures between roughly −150°C and 2,000°C give off thermal radiation, predominantly of infrared light. This infrared light is not visible to the human eye, so we do not see these objects glowing. We can, however, often feel this light as it is absorbed by our skin, warming it up.

There are electronic devices that can sense infrared light. This makes it possible to build cameras that can "see" the temperature of objects, by measuring the infrared light that they emit. This kind of temperature detection is called thermography.

Infrared light is also used in "night-vision" sensors. At night, the sun no longer provides light to reflect off of objects. Because the objects are warm, however (around room temperature for objects or body temperature for people), they emit their own infrared light without needing a source such as the sun. This makes it possible for infrared-detecting equipment to "see" at night.

and cold areas, by displaying which kind of infrared light the objects are giving off.

Furthermore, human skin easily absorbs infrared light. This heats up the skin and you perceive warmth. When you can feel the heat of an oven or a fireplace from some distance, much of what you are feeling is the absorption of the infrared light that was emitted as thermal radiation.

HEAT AND CHEMISTRY

In the next chapter, we will explore the origin of chemical energy. This is the energy that, for instance, powers your car from the chemical energy of gasoline, or powers you from the chemical energy of your food. Chemical energy is often made useful by transforming it into thermal energy and heat, as in combustion. This transformation increases temperatures and can be further used to produce useful work, subject to the Carnot limit on extracting work from heat.

HEAT CAPACITY

When heat is transferred to an object, the object's temperature increases. Conversely, when heat flows out of an object, the object's temperature decreases. By how much does the temperature of the object change as heat moves in or out?

The **specific heat capacity** of a material is how much heat it takes to raise the temperature 1 degree Celsius (or kelvin—remember, they are the same size) per kilogram of mass. Why is it called heat capacity? Well, think of a suitcase with a large capacity—you can put a lot into it without distorting the shape of the suitcase. On the other hand, if you try to stuff two weeks' worth of clothes into your backpack, it will become overstuffed and greatly distorted. Similarly, when a material has high heat capacity, you can add a lot of heat without changing the temperature very much—that is, without distorting it much. An object with low heat capacity, on the other hand, changes its temperature (distorts) much more for the same amount of heat.

You might notice that water has a very high heat capacity. This is a very important fact. It explains why the weather and breezes are so different at a beach near the ocean than inland. It is also why humid summer nights stay so warm, while desert nights (with very little water in the air) change temperature so dramatically. It is also why, whenever possible, water is used as a coolant. It does not heat rapidly, so even after absorbing a lot of heat, it can stay cold and continue to act as a coolant.

THE SUN'S HEAT

Light from the Sun is constantly transferring energy from the Sun to the Earth. A 1 m^2 collector plate on the space shuttle that is facing the Sun could receive 1,500 watts of energy from sunlight. On Earth, we may receive less than one-third as much energy per

Cooling a Car Engine

As we've described, a car must operate part of its system at very high temperatures in order to get a high efficiency despite the Carnot limit. Part of the system, however, must also operate at low temperature. Unfortunately, the hot parts tend to heat up the cold parts, reducing the temperature difference between them. This is why a car has a coolant system designed to pull excess heat energy away from parts of the engine.

The coolant system consists of three major parts: a liquid coolant, a pump, and a radiator. The liquid coolant is a mix of water and anti-freeze. Anti-freeze is usually made primarily of the chemical ethylene glycol, which not only protects the water from freezing at low temperatures, it also protects the water from boiling at high temperatures. It is not only anti-freeze but anti-boil.

The pump moves the water through the parts of the engine that need to be cooled. As these parts can warm the water well over 100°C (the usual boiling point of water), it is essential that the antifreeze has been added. The water flows over the hot parts of the engine and heat is transferred by conduction from the engine to the flowing water. The heat is transferred because the water is cooler than the parts—heat, as always, flows from hot to cold.

The water, now heated up, flows to the radiator. This is an example of water flowing by convection, in this case, carried by the water. The water, now hot, contacts the radiator. The radiator consists of a very long, thin tube snaking its way through a mesh. As the car moves forward, air flows over the mesh. This airflow, in turn, carries heat away from the mesh, keeping the mesh cool. Because the mesh is relatively cool, it carries the heat away from the metal tube that the water is flowing through.

In the process as a whole, heat flows by conduction from engine to water, by convection from there to the radiator, then heat flows by conduction from the flowing water to the tube. The heat flows by conduction from the tube to the mesh to the air, and then by convection in the air, away from the car. The net result is to pass heat from the engine to heat the air that is around your car.

square meter because of the time of day, the inclination of the Sun, and reflection and absorption of light by the atmosphere. To get an idea of how much energy 1,500 watts is, we can compare it to power transfers of equal size:

- A lawnmower cutting blade uses this much power to cut grass every second.
- This much power can heat one kilogram of water 0.24°C every second.
- This is the same power as dropping one water balloon per second from a height of 222 meters.
- This is the same power as two strong horses at maximum power output.
- The total power used in an average household every day is about 1,500 watts. We cannot, however, easily change all the sunlight power delivered to our solar collector into useful power for the house.

CHAPTER 5

Electrical Energy of an AA Battery: 8 Watt-Hours

OFTEN IN THE WINTER, AFTER WALKING AROUND FOR A while, you collect "static electricity"—an electrical **charge** builds up on you. Atoms are made of electrons (with negative charge) and **protons** (positively charged), and under normal circumstances objects have the same number of electrons as protons, and hence a total electrical charge of zero. Static electricity is a rather unfortunate name—it simply means electrical charge. When you have static electricity, it means that your body has more electrons than protons. This, in turn, means that the total electrical charge is no longer zero.

Static electricity can happen as you walk across a carpet— electrons are rubbed off the carpet and onto yourself. It actually takes energy for this to happen, although you do not notice it. While walking across the floor, heat from the friction of your shoes rubbing against the carpet is enough to detach the electrons from the carpet.

This is a useful place for us to review potential energy. Remember, the potential energy difference between two configurations is due to work that was done in the past against a force. Since it requires energy to detach electrons from their atoms in the carpet, when, where, and by whom was this work done, and against what force?

First, the final configuration (with extra electrons on you rather than on the carpet) requires energy to be put in. This is like the pencil on the floor. You must do work to lift the pencil from the floor, just as here you must do work to detach the electron from the atoms in the carpet.

With the pencil, lifting it from the floor requires work due to the force of gravity. The work has to be done to the object as you lift, because the force of gravity is directed oppositely (downward) to the direction in which you are moving (upward). Of course, since you are providing the force to lift it, the force is directed upward in the same direction as the displacement; so the work you do is positive. The total work you did, which is the change in the potential difference, depends on the change in the height by which you lifted it (Δh):

$$\Delta PE = mg\Delta h$$

What is the force that acts against detaching the electron from the atom in the carpet as gravity works against lifting a pencil from the floor? In this case, the acting force is the electrical force. Most likely, you have heard that "opposites attract" and "like repels like." These two statements are about the directions of electrical forces. The electrical force between two electrical charges acts either to repel or attract them. With electrons in atoms, the positively charged protons in the nucleus attract the electron, just as the Earth's gravity attracts the pencil. So, to pull the electron away from the atom requires you to do work, just as pulling the pencil away from the Earth (lifting it) requires work (Figure 5.1).

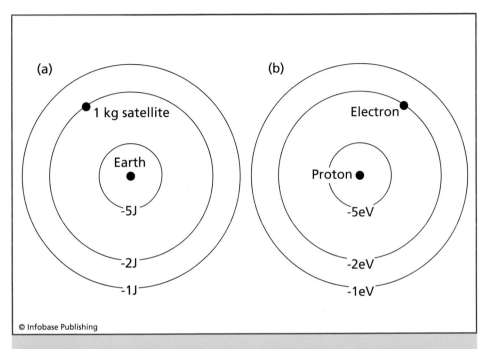

Figure 5.1 *(a) The attractive force of gravity attracts a 1 kg object; moving the object away from the Earth increases the potential energy, and moving it toward the Earth decreases the potential energy. (b) The attractive electrical force between a proton and an electron: When pulling them apart, the potential increases; when they come together, the potential decreases.*

Of course, once you have lifted the pencil, having done your work, the pencil has potential energy. You can recover this potential energy (in the form of kinetic energy, or work) by returning it to the original configuration (for example, by dropping the pencil, or lowering it to the floor). Is it the same with the electrons that have collected on you as you walked across the floor? Since energy is conserved, it must be.

The most common way to recover this energy is through a "spark." This usually comes when you touch a metal object like a doorknob or water faucet. The jolt that you feel, and the spark that comes with it, is the release of the stored electrical potential energy.

When negative and positive charges become separated, so that the total charge is no longer zero, there is going to likely be electrical potential energy. What is the "base" configuration (like the pencil on the floor)?

The easiest way to define electrical potential energy would be to take the base configuration as all the charges together making a net charge of zero. For instance, an electron and proton together (making a hydrogen atom) would have potential energy of zero. If you managed to pull them apart (by doing work against the attractive force of electricity), then the potential energy of the pulled-apart configuration would be positive. Unfortunately, for reasons beyond the scope of this text, this is not how electrical potential is usually based. Instead, the base configuration is defined as the configuration with the electron and proton pulled completely apart, with a large (infinite) distance between them.

Remember, it doesn't matter how you define the base configuration—the difference between two configurations is the same regardless, which you call zero. For instance, if the base configuration is the pencil on the floor, the pencil on your desk might have a potential energy of +1 J. If instead you define the pencil on your desk as the base of zero, then the pencil on the floor would have a potential energy of –1 J. In either case, the potential energy on the desk is 1 J higher than the potential energy on the floor.

Let us imagine any configuration of electron and proton where they are not separated by an infinite distance—that means they came closer together. The force between them is attractive. So, like gravity, if you move in the direction the force desires (downward, in the case of gravity), the potential is lower. The potential energy of the pencil on the floor is lower than the energy of the pencil on the desk because it has gone in the same direction as the force. So, any other configuration than full separation has a potential energy lower than the base. Which is to say, all electrical potential energies between opposite charges are negative compared to full separation. To be sure you understand, answer this question: Are all electrical potential energies between same-sign charges positive or negative?

Of course, not all electrical potential energy *differences* are negative! If you move between one configuration with a certain separation, and another with a different separation, the potential energy difference between these two may be positive or negative.

ELECTRICITY

We are not going to explain all of **electricity** here but only the barest facts, enough to understand energy. When we want to discuss electrical charges, we need some way to quantify the amount of electric charge. That is, in the same way that kilograms quantify the amount of mass, meters quantify the amount of distance, or seconds quantify the amount of time. The best way to quantify electrical charge would be to simply count the number of electrons (or protons) and just record that number. So, we would say "there are 3×10^{12} electrons' charge." If the charge were positive, we would say "there are 3×10^{12} protons' charge" or "-3×10^{12} electrons' charge."

Unfortunately, this easily understood way of quantifying charge is not the standard method. When scientists first studied electricity in the seventeenth and eighteenth centuries, they did not know about electrons and protons. So, they defined the "coulomb" unit (named after French physicist Charles de Coulomb). A **coulomb** (C) consists of the charge of 6.2×10^{18} protons.

In electricity, we usually discuss not the electrical potential energy, but the electrical potential. Electrical potential is the potential energy of a charged object divided by the object's charge. Like gravitational potential energy we are most often interested in the difference in electric potential between two positions of an object. Electrical potential differences are measured in joules/coulomb. This makes potential differences different from potential energy, given simply in joules. This is because electrical potential energy depends on the number of coulombs (Figure 5.2).

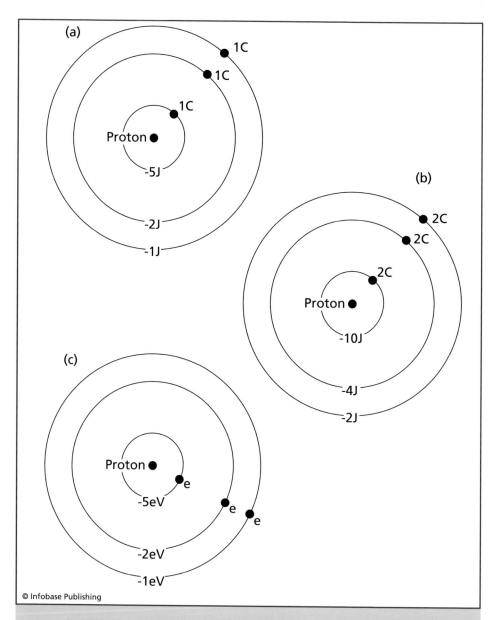

Figure 5.2 *(a) Electrical potential energy (as a function of distance) for a proton attracting 1 C of charge. (b) Electrical potential energy for a proton attracting 2 C of charge. (c) Electrical potential energy for a proton attracting 1 electron.*

The electrical potential is used because it tells us how much energy we would have to provide to move a charge from one place to another. In many common situations, the electrical potential is an unchanging factor. Therefore, moving a charge of 3 coulombs through a potential difference of 5 joules/coulomb requires 15 joules of energy. Moving a charge of 30 coulombs through the same potential difference requires 150 joules of energy. Usually, by moving these charges, the electrical potential (in joules/coulomb) does not change. So, the next transfer of charge from one place to another has the same electrical potential difference, but not necessarily the same electrical potential energy difference, if the number of coulombs is different (Figure 5.3).

One joule/coulomb has another name, the **volt** (V). So, a 9-volt battery is one in which every coulomb of charge moving from the plus side to the minus side acquires 9 joules. Two coulombs moving from the plus to the minus side would acquire 18 joules. The volt is defined such that the change in potential energy ΔE depends on the charge q and the voltage difference ΔV:

$$\Delta E = q \Delta V$$

An electron completely separated from a proton has an electrical potential of 0 volts. If the electron is brought closer to the proton, its electrical potential will be negative (as discussed earlier). It might be, for instance, −1 volts. This means that the amount of work that could have been done by the charge in moving to its new position, closer to the proton, is

$$\Delta E = q \Delta V = -1.6 \times 10^{-19}\,C \times -1V = -1.6 \times 10^{-19}\,C \times -1J\,/\,C = -1.6 \times 10^{-19}\,J$$

This energy—one electron charge moving through one volt—is important enough to have its own name: the electron volt (eV). One eV is equivalent to 1.6×10^{-19} J.

Electron volts are quite small units of energy. They are often used to describe the energies in atoms and molecules, which are all held together by electrostatic forces. In a hydrogen atom, the

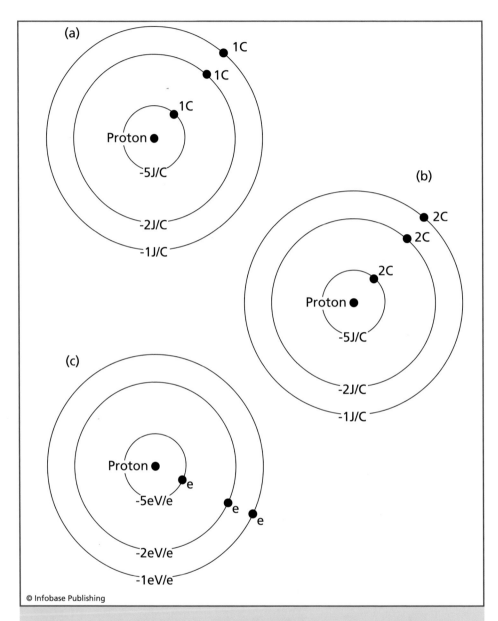

Figure 5.3 *The electrical potential energy, divided by the number of coulombs. The electrical potential of the proton is the same, even though the electrical potential energy* is different.

electron orbits the proton in a way such that the potential energy of the electron is −13.6 eV. That means that one would have to add +13.6 eV of energy to the electron to pull it far away from the proton. This energy is the electrical binding energy of a single proton and a single electron (because it would take this much energy to separate them back out very far apart). And what is the electrical potential? The energy is

$$13.6eV = 13.6eV \times \frac{1\frac{J}{C}}{V} \times \frac{1.6 \times 10^{-19}C}{e} = 2.2 \times 10^{-18} J$$

The electrical potential difference is the energy difference divided by the charge involved; here, that charge is one electron, or 1.6×10^{-19} C:

$$\Delta V = \frac{2.2 \times 10^{-18} J}{1.6 \times 10^{-19} C} = 13.6V$$

So, the electric potential is −13.6 V. Remember, the binding energy is −13.6 eV. The e is all-important.

The outlets in your home, if you live in the United States, have a voltage difference of 110 volts. What does this mean? It means that if you tried to move one positive coulomb of charge from the negative side to the positive side, the amount of work done by the charge to move it would be:

$$W = -q\Delta V = -(1C \times +110V) = -(1C \times 110J/C) = -110J$$

On the other side (and, the more usual and useful side), if you are moving 1 C of charge from the positive side to the negative side, this charge can do a positive amount of work:

$$W = -q\Delta V = -(1C \times -110V) = +110J$$

This is work that you can use for whatever purpose you have in mind. That might be 110 joules of energy to spin a cooling fan, heat a cup of coffee, or light up a computer monitor.

PHYSICS AND PEOPLE: Batteries

You probably have a cell phone that you carry with you, an iPod or CD player, and perhaps a laptop computer. At home, you probably have remote controls to control the TV, DVD, and stereo. All of these portable devices hinge on crucial advances in energy storage. In particular, on advances in battery technology. We rarely give much thought to the four AA batteries we pop into a device, but without good batteries, portable devices are useless.

By energy storage, we mean potential energy that came from doing work at some time in the past, which can be conveniently released whenever we like. So, somehow we had to do work to get energy into the battery; and then we can carry the battery around and release the energy later. The energy in a battery does not come for free.

The crucial parameter for a battery is how much electrical energy it can store up in one kilogram of mass (Table 5.1).

TABLE 5.1 Energy Storage per Weight for Different Batteries			
	g	J	J/kg
Alkaline	24	9,360	390,000
Carbon-Zinc	19	2,340	123,158
NiCad	29	4,320	148,966
NiMH	26	9,072	348,923
Lithium Ion	24	11,050	460,417
Lead-Acid	10,000	1,440,000	144,000

Let's look at the signs a moment because they're important. The change in potential energy is

$$\Delta E = q\Delta V$$

But if we look back at our table of signs in chapter 3, we see that potential energy change of an object, and the work done by the object, always have an opposite sign $\Delta E = -W$. So:

$$W = -q\Delta V$$

BATTERIES, CARS, AND TRUMPETS

An AA battery typically has the stored energy of 8 watt-hours. How much is a watt-hour? We can convert the units to find

$$8Wh = 8Wh \times \frac{3,600s}{1h} = 28,800Ws = 28,800J$$

This is because 1 watt of power for a time of 1 second produces 1 joule of energy, So this battery stores up 28,800 J.

Since many AA batteries are dedicated to powering devices that we listen to, it is interesting to note that sound takes relatively little energy to make. Sound is a vibration of air, and vibrating air molecules, since they are moving back and forth, must contain kinetic energy. So, it takes energy to create sound. Because our ears are extremely sensitive, they require very little energy in the sound in order for us to hear it.

The amount of energy in an AA battery is equivalent to:

- a 1,000 kg car moving at 27 kilometers per hour
- the potential energy of a 1,000 kg car lifted 3 meters into the air on a hydraulic lift
- the energy needed to boil a quarter cup of water from room temperature

- the energy transferred by sunlight to a 1 m² area in 20 seconds
- the energy needed to lift a dust mite to escape velocity
- average household electrical use for 15 seconds
- the sound energy of a trumpet playing for 24 hours.

You could use an AA battery to power your house for 15 seconds. Not very much energy in each one, is there?

CHAPTER 6

Chemical Energy of 1 Kilogram of Sugar: 17 Million Joules

CHEMISTRY IS THE STUDY OF WHAT HAPPENS WHEN ELECtrons change their configurations around nuclei. In general, any changes in the nuclei themselves fall into the field of nuclear physics. Given a configuration of nuclei, chemists try to determine how the electrons arrange themselves and what the potential energy of the configuration is.

As electrons and protons are attracted by electrical forces, this study of **chemical energy** is really the deep and detailed study of electrical potential energy. Although at first it may simply seem just another application of electrical potential energy, it is of such overwhelming practical importance, and so intricate due to the interplay of electricity and quantum mechanics, that it deserves a separate discussion.

ENERGY LEVELS IN CHEMICALS

An electron and a proton together form the simplest chemical—hydrogen. As we discussed in the previous chapter, a single electron and a single proton have the lowest possible potential energy,

–13.6 eV. The electron cannot come closer to the proton to lower its potential even further due to the effects of quantum mechanics. The electron-proton pair can have potential energies between 0 (pulled completely apart) and –13.6 eV. Not all values between 0 and –13.6 eV, however, are possible.

The electron-proton pair, a hydrogen atom, can only choose out of a set of possible potential energies. This is different from, for instance, the usual understanding of gravity. Your pencil can have zero potential energy on the floor, or 0.01 J while one centimeter above the floor, or 0.00001 J while one micrometer above the floor. Not so with an electron and a proton. Only certain potential energy levels are allowed: –13.6 eV, –3.4 eV, –1.51 eV, –0.85 eV, –0.54 eV, etc. In fact, the potential energies that are allowed follow this pattern:

$$PE = -\frac{13.6eV}{n^2}$$

The quantity n can be any integer. When $n = 1$, that is the lowest allowed level, called the **ground state**. When $n = 2$, it is the next lowest level, and so on. Notice that as n gets larger and larger, the potential energy gets closer and closer to 0—that is, the separation gets larger and larger.

So, instead of simply lifting our pencil, now we are only allowed to put it on a shelf. The shelves of a hydrogen atom's electron energy levels are arranged somewhat as in Figure 6.1 If we move the electron downward from a shelf, the energy we can get from that corresponds to the difference in energy levels; if we move the electron upward, we must add to the electron exactly the amount of energy difference between those levels. If we try to impart 1 eV to an electron on the second shelf of (a) the electron will not move. There is no shelf at –2.4 eV to receive the electron.

This being the case for hydrogen atoms, how do atoms with more protons and electrons behave? Qualitatively, they behave the same way. For a given set of protons and a given number of electrons, the rules of electricity, combined with the rules of quantum mechanics, define a set of energy levels that are possible. When

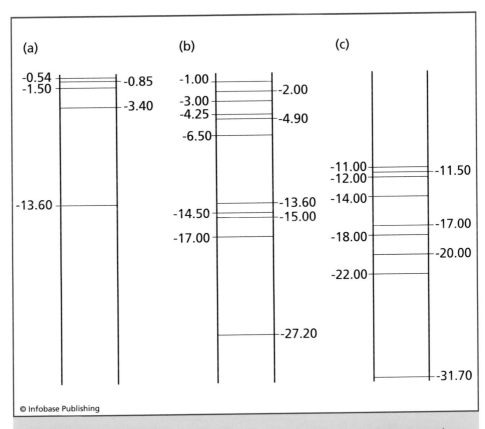

(a)

-0.54
-1.50
-0.85

-3.40

-13.60

(b)

-1.00
-2.00

-3.00
-4.25
-4.90

-6.50

-14.50
-13.60
-15.00

-17.00

-27.20

(c)

-11.00
-12.00
-11.50

-14.00

-18.00

-22.00

-17.00

-20.00

-31.70

© Infobase Publishing

Figure 6.1 *(a) The electrical potential energies that are possible when a proton and electron come together, displayed as a shelf analogous to the gravitational potential energy. The lowest shelf is called the "ground state." (b) The electrical potential energies that are possible with two protons and two electrons, when each electron-proton pair is separated by a large distance. The ground state is twice as low as in (a). (c) The electrical potential energy values that are possible when the two pairs of electron and proton are brought near each other. Notice that the ground state has now moved to a lower value.*

the number of electrons is equal to the number of protons in the nucleus, there is always a lowest energy level ground state, with negative energy, which indicates that the electrons are bound to the nucleus. There are then a variety of levels, with energy between the ground state and zero. Again, transitions can only occur between one level and another one.

CHEMICAL BONDS

What about the levels for molecules with multiple atoms? Perhaps you will not be surprised that the same behavior also holds true for a system consisting of multiple atoms. There is a ground state, with the lowest possible energy, and additional states higher in energy (but still negative). When multiple atoms come together, however, something altogether profound happens. To understand it, we return to the proton and electron.

When the proton and electron were separated, they had a potential of 0 V. After coming together, they had a potential energy of –13.6 eV, called the binding energy. Similarly, imagine we have one hydrogen atom very far separated from another hydrogen atom. Each one has a potential energy of –13.6 eV (compared to having itself pulled apart). When the two hydrogen atoms come together, what is the total binding energy? A good guess would be twice the binding energy of each hydrogen atom—that is, –27.2 eV. But instead it is –31.7 eV.

This probably strikes you as a petty numerical detail, but it is not at all. It is the very reason it is possible for you, the Earth, and everything on it to exist. When two hydrogen atoms come together, they have a total potential energy *even lower* than two separated single hydrogen atoms. When the atoms come together, the electrons are able to "move closer" to the protons than possible when the atoms are apart. The total energy of the atoms nearby to one another is therefore lower.

This means that as they come together, they must release energy. And that, of course, means that to pull them apart again, we would have to supply more energy. So this difference, of 4.5 eV, is the binding energy of two hydrogen atoms that come together. They end up bound together into a hydrogen molecule. This is a chemical bond (Figure 6.2).

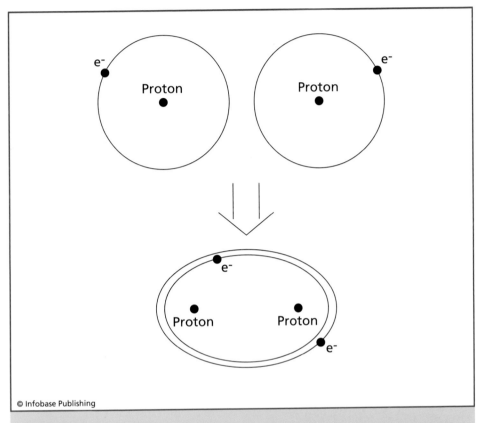

© Infobase Publishing

Figure 6.2 *As two atoms come together, a new possibility emerges for a lower ground state. As the electrons of the atoms fall into this lower ground state, it releases energy, and the atoms become bound. It would require this much energy to separate them again. We say these two atoms have a "chemical bond."*

To restate what happened: If two hydrogen atoms are separated by a wide distance, you would have to do 27.2 eV of work to separate them into two protons and two electrons. But if you bring the two hydrogen atoms together, they will release more energy, and it will take 31.7 eV to separate them all into two electrons and two atoms. It would take 4.5 eV just to separate them back into two hydrogen atoms.

EXPLORING CHEMICAL BONDS

Each hydrogen atom is electrically neutral (one electron, one proton). What is the force between them that is giving rise to this potential energy? It is an electrical force. The energy levels of atoms change when they come together and, in general, the lowest energy level will be even lower once the atoms come together. This is the very essence of what makes chemistry (and therefore, biology) possible.

We can bring many different kinds of atoms together: hydrogen together with carbon, nitrogen with sulfur, oxygen with chlorine. We are interested in the lowest energy ground state of the atoms separately, and then together. The difference in ground state energy as they are brought together is the binding energy of the pair. This difference can either be calculated using advanced techniques or directly measured. Table 6.1 shows a set of measured binding energies for a variety of atom pair bonds.

Note, for instance, that a chemical bond between one hydrogen atom and one carbon atom has binding energy of 4.3 eV. Table 6.1 is for single chemical bonds; so-called "double" and "triple" bonds, which you may have learned about in chemistry class, generally have higher binding energy.

The strengths of these various bonds dictate what chemical reactions are possible and whether the reactions are **exothermic** (releasing heat energy when the reaction takes place) or **endothermic** (consuming heat energy). Exothermic reactions may or may not happen spontaneously, depending on the details of the reaction energies. Endothermic reactions almost never happen spontaneously—they require energy to be input first. Sometimes, however, endothermic reactions can acquire their energy from heat energy in the environment. An endothermic chemical reaction absorbs heat from its surroundings and therefore the chemical can feel cooler to the touch. Athletic trainers often use hot packs or cold packs to treat bruises or sprains. These packages are filled with chemicals that undergo, respectively, exothermic or endothermic reactions.

TABLE 6.1 **Binding Energies (in eV) of Chemical Bonds**

	Cl	F	O	N	C	H
H	4.5	5.8	4.8	4.1	4.3	4.5
C	3.4	4.6	3.6	3.0	3.6	
N	2.1	2.8	1.8	1.7		
O	2.1	1.9	1.4			
F	2.6	1.6				
Cl	2.5					

In general, chemical reactions release their excess energy as heat rather than as work. At first, this may seem puzzling. After all, electrical potential energy can easily be converted to work, and often is, with full efficiency without considering the temperature. Since chemical potential energy is a form of electrical potential energy, why is it released as heat (which is subject to the Carnot limit) rather than work?

The reason is because the energy released in chemical reactions is almost always initially released as a form of light, often infrared, but also possibly ultraviolet (UV), visible, or even microwave. In general, however, the reaction takes place inside a liquid or solid, and the light cannot travel very far before it is absorbed and changed into thermal motion of molecules.

When the light is absorbed or reflected, it increases the energy of whatever molecule it has hit. This could cause the molecule to recoil as it was hit or it could cause one of the electrons to temporarily gain in potential energy (leap to a higher shelf). Eventually, the electron would fall back down to the lowest shelf, but often it will do so not in a single leap back down (as it did coming up) but in multiple small downward steps. By moving downward this way, the energy of the original light would be spread out randomly into more lower-energy light. This light may in turn reflect or be absorbed, exciting additional molecules, or causing them to recoil.

In this way, inside the liquid or solid where the reaction takes place, the energy released in the reaction rapidly diffuses out into random molecule kinetic energy (from recoils) and low-energy light (from excitation followed by de-excitation). This random energy, spread out through the liquid or solid, is a form of thermal energy, and can be extracted from the reactants only as heat, rather than work.

THE ENERGY OF SUGARS

Plants use the light of the Sun in order to turn carbon dioxide and water into glucose, a kind of sugar. Glucose has a higher (more positive) potential energy than the carbon dioxide and water; this also means if the glucose is broken down into its components, energy is released.

Why do plants do this? Making glucose is equivalent to lifting a weight up to a higher place. If later you need energy, you can lower the weight and use it to release potential energy as it moves to lower potential. In the same way, the glucose, because it is at higher potential energy, stores energy that can be released later. Plants store the energy of sunlight in the higher potential energy of glucose.

Glucose releases energy through the chemical reaction:

$$C_6H_{12}O_6 + 6O_2 = 6CO_2 + 6H_2O + 62 \text{ eV}$$

The chemical formula for glucose is $C_6H_{12}O_6$; oxygen in the air is O_2. This is the chemical process in the cells of your body that provides their energy. You breathe in O_2 and breathe out CO_2 (carbon dioxide), and emit H_2O in various ways (for instance, by evaporation of sweat). This process releases energy, which your body uses to keep warm, to keep your organs working, and to do physical work. The process is made possible because of the positive potential energy in the glucose, the 62 eV. Of course, 62 eV by itself—the energy from a single glucose reaction—is very small. On the other hand, it happens to quadrillions of glucose molecules every second in your body, and that adds up to the energy you use.

In fact, in one kilogram of table sugar, all these molecules add up to provide an energy of 17 million joules (MJ). Just how much energy is this? It is equal to:

- the electrical energy in 600 AA batteries
- the potential energy stored in Liberty's torch, arm, and head
- the chemical energy in 0.4 kg of gasoline
- the kinetic energy of a 1,000 kg car going 644 kilometers per hour
- the energy required to launch a baseball to escape velocity
- the energy to power the electricity in most households for 3 hours
- the energy needed to boil 38 liters of water from room temperature
- the energy needed for a 45 kg human to climb a mountain 38 kilometers high.

Compared to, for instance, AA batteries or hoisting giant weights very high into the air, you should be impressed with how much chemical energy is stored in 1 kg of sugar. The chemical energy stored in gasoline is even more impressive. Remember, however, that this energy is always expressed as heat. For this reason, it is subject to the Carnot limit in how much useful work (or mechanical energy) can be extracted from it. Very high temperatures are needed to be efficient at using this heat as work. Car engines are designed to run very hot for this reason. Although the total potential heat in 1 kg of sugar is 17 million joules, the usable portion (for a warm-blooded human) of this is only enough to climb a mountain about 1 kilometer high.

CHAPTER 7

Relativistic Energy of 1 Kilogram of Helium Fusion: 270 Trillion Joules

E ARLIER, WE LEARNED THAT THE KINETIC ENERGY OF A moving object is

$$KE = \frac{1}{2}mv^2$$

One hundred years ago, however, Albert Einstein (Figure 7.1) wrote his paper on **relativity**, in which he demonstrated that when objects approach the speed of light, $1/2mv^2$ is not a good expression for the kinetic energy. It becomes increasingly inaccurate as an object moves faster. It is, of course, rather accurate for cases when the velocity (v) is much smaller than the speed of light.

In fact, Einstein found a new expression for the energy of a moving object. For an object moving fast-but-not-too-fast compared to the speed of light (c), the new expression can be written as:

$$E = mc^2 + \frac{1}{2}mv^2 + \frac{3}{8}m\frac{v^4}{c^2}$$

Figure 7.1 *In 1905, Albert Einstein produced three groundbreaking papers that revolutionized physics, transforming our conceptions of light, space, and time.*

If you look at this formula for a while, you will notice three things about it. First, it does have a $1/2mv^2$ in it, just like kinetic energy—after all, the kinetic energy is pretty accurate for velocities we have used before. Second, you will notice there is an extra term $3/8mv^4/c^2$ that includes velocity.

How fast must an object be going in order for the new term to change the energy calculation by 1%? It turns out the object must be going 40 million meters per second—or about 90 million miles per hour. The fastest man-made object to date is the Helios 1 satellite, which travels at about 158,000 miles per hour. At this "slow" speed, the kinetic energy correction due to the third term of the formula is less than one part in a million. So, even for the fastest man-made objects, the usual $1/2mv^2$ term is adequate for accuracy, without Einstein's third term.

The third thing about the formula, of course, is that there is a famous first term of mc^2. Just to be clear, imagine an object which is not moving at all: $v = 0$. Then, you see that $E = mc^2$, the most famous statement of this new equation, only holds for objects that are not moving!

So, now let's look at our formula again:

$$E = mc^2 + \frac{1}{2}mv^2 + \frac{3}{8}m\frac{v^4}{c^2}$$

We have found that the third term is nearly always negligible compared to the first two. In fact, only in high-energy particle physics is it needed. So, for objects that you normally see, Einstein's equation reduces to

$$E = mc^2 + \frac{1}{2}mv^2$$

The student who has been paying close attention will object at this point. When we do work, it changes the kinetic energy. Changing potentials also changes the kinetic energy. Since we look at kinetic energy differences when energy transfers, it doesn't really matter whether:

$$E = mc^2 + \frac{1}{2}mv^2$$

or

$$E = \frac{1}{2}mv^2$$

because mc^2 is a constant. When you take the difference, it cancels out. For instance, a 1kg object going 2 m/s has energy:

$$E_2 = 1kg \times \left(3 \times 10^8 \frac{m}{s}\right)^2 + \frac{1}{2} \times 1kg \times \left(2\frac{m}{s}\right)^2$$

An object going 4 m/s has energy:

$$E_4 = 1kg \times \left(3 \times 10^8 \frac{m}{s}\right)^2 + \frac{1}{2} \times 1kg \times \left(4\frac{m}{s}\right)^2$$

The difference is:

$$E_2 - E_4 = \frac{1}{2} \times 1kg \times 12\frac{m^2}{s^2}$$

This is exactly the same change as if we had not used Einstein's formula, and instead only used the original formula for kinetic energies:

$$E_2 = \frac{1}{2} \times 1kg \times \left(2\frac{m}{s}\right)^2$$

and

$$E_4 = \frac{1}{2} \times 1kg \times \left(4\frac{m}{s}\right)^2$$

So, what is the point of the extra complication of adding a constant to the energy of a moving object? If the mass of objects cannot change, there is no point. Einstein's equation, however, allows us to investigate situations in which the mass of the object changes, such as when an atomic nucleus splits in a nuclear power reactor. In such a case, we find that some of the mass of the nucleus has disappeared in the reaction. Where does the mass go and what is the effect of the loss?

As an example what would happen if we could change the mass of a 1 kg object into a 0.999 kg one. How much energy is equivalent to the lost 0.001 kg? The energy of the original object would be

$$E = mc^2 + 0 = 1kg \times \left(3 \times 10^8 \frac{m}{s}\right)^2 = 9.0 \times 10^{16} J$$

And the energy of the new, slightly lighter object, would be

$$E = mc^2 + 0 = 0.999kg \times \left(3 \times 10^8 \frac{m}{s}\right)^2 = 8.991 \times 10^{16} J$$

The difference is 9×10^{13} J, a hefty amount of energy.

Is energy conserved? Yes, if there is kinetic energy released as a result of this reduction in mass. In most such reactions, the kinetic energy is spread out among several final components, not one single object. But let us calculate what the final velocity of this object would be if all the 9×10^{13} J were invested in moving the object. In order for the energy to be conserved,

$$\frac{1}{2}mv^2 = 9 \times 10^{13} J$$

$$v = \sqrt{\frac{2 \times 9 \times 10^{13} J}{0.999kg}} = 13.4 \times 10^6 \frac{m}{s}$$

So, if we could reduce the weight of an object by 0.1%, it would produce enough energy to propel the object to a velocity of millions of meters per second! That would be much, much faster than the fastest rocket ever built.

You've probably learned about conservation of momentum; in the calculation above, we started with one object at rest and ended with a lightened object moving. This is not allowed by the laws of physics. Let us correct this by letting the new, lighter object split in two, moving in opposite directions (Figure 7.2), with each carrying half of the energy. So, for each half:

$$\frac{1}{2}mv^2 = 4.5 \times 10^{13} J$$
$$v = 13.4 \times 10^6 J$$

It really does not change the final velocity whichever way you calculate it. If we could find a reaction in which the mass is reduced, we could use it to propel masses to very high velocities for only a very small change in the mass (0.1%).

When you come across large and surprising numbers like this, you should always ask yourself, "How did the number come out so large?" This is to be sure you have not made a mistake in the calculation. In this case, the number is so large because c, the speed of light, is so large. Especially if you multiply by 0.1%, the square of the speed of light is a mighty big number.

On to the big question: How do you reduce the mass of something?

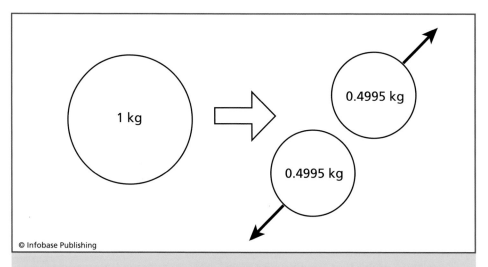

Figure 7.2 *An object originally at left reduces its total mass by 0.1% as it splits into two pieces; these two pieces fly off at very high speeds as the energy of the mass is converted to kinetic energy.*

STRONG FORCES AND BINDING ENERGY

As we saw earlier, the attractive electrical force between an electron and a proton leads to the binding energy of a hydrogen atom. Recall the binding energy is the energy required to separate the proton and electron completely, and this energy was released (as light or heat) when the proton and electron were brought together.

The different chemical elements consist of nuclei with different numbers of protons in the nucleus. For instance, hydrogen contains one proton; helium has two protons, and gold has 79 protons. The number of **neutrons** does not change the chemical element; the most common hydrogen atoms have no neutrons; the most common helium atoms have two neutrons; and the most common gold atoms have 118 neutrons.

It is puzzling that protons can all be tightly packed into the **nucleus**. After all, they should repel each other electrically: like repels like! How is it possible that the protons stay stuck together in the nucleus, rather than repelling and flying apart? There must be some additional attractive force that holds them together, and this force must be stronger than the electrical force. Because this force only appears to operate in the nucleus, and because it is stronger than the electrical force, it is (unimaginatively, but descriptively) called the **strong nuclear force**.

The next question is: When two protons are attracted by the strong force, do they also release binding energy as they come together? It will come as no surprise to you to learn that they do. Just how much energy do they release as they are attracted together?

FUSION, FISSION, AND BINDING ENERGY

Figure 7.3 shows the amount of binding energy present for atoms with an **atomic number** (the number of protons) from 1 to 92. The binding energy is the potential energy due to all of the attractive strong nuclear forces and the repulsive electric forces among all the protons and neutrons in the nucleus. When free protons and neutrons combine to make a nucleus, their kinetic energies are transformed into potential energy. This nuclear binding energy is so large in magnitude that it affects the mass of the nucleus through the $E = mc^2$ term. By changing a nucleus from one number to another, we might be able to change the total binding energy, reduce the mass by an amount Δm and release the energy difference equal to Δmc^2.

One example of how this works is in the **fusion** of nuclei that occurs in the Sun. This reaction includes a special form of hydrogen called deuterium, which has one extra neutron. In the hot environment of the Sun, one deuterium nucleus (one proton and one neutron) can fuse with one hydrogen nucleus (one proton) to produce one helium nucleus (^{3}He, two protons, one neutron). The total mass of the new ^{3}He nucleus is about 1×10^{-29} kg less than the sum of the masses of the proton and deuterium nuclei. Where did this mass go? The fused particles became more tightly bound in the new nucleus and released energy. It escaped as light energy equivalent to 5.5×10^6 eV. This is part of the energy that heats the Earth.

From the graph of binding energies, you can see that as you combine larger and larger nuclei beyond helium, the binding energy becomes more negative until you make an iron nucleus. Fusing two nuclei smaller than iron will produce a larger, more tightly bound nucleus, and energy will be released. On the other hand, if you combine nuclei larger than iron, they are less tightly bound. They will not fuse unless you add energy to them.

To make heavy nuclei release energy, you must break them into pieces. This process is called **fission**. For instance, radioactive uranium can spontaneously break up into two or more smaller nuclei. These nuclei are each more tightly bound and have less total mass than the original uranium nucleus. The lost mass is expelled as light energy or kinetic energy of the nuclei. This fission process is one used to produce heat in a commercial nuclear power plant.

The hydrogen fusion reaction and uranium fission reactions are attractive not only because they produce large amounts of energy, but they also have low activation energies, and therefore the reactions can be self-sustaining. As with fire, once energy release is started, it can provide the activation energy for even more

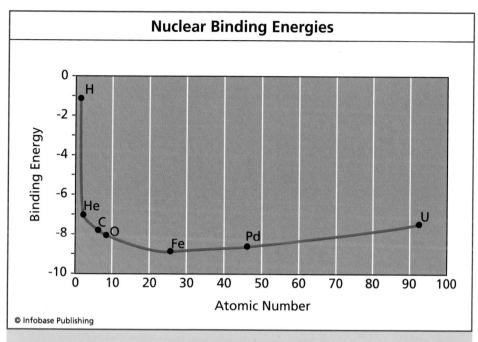

Figure 7.3 *Binding energy as a function of atomic number. The lowest atomic number is 1 for hydrogen; the largest depicted here is 92 for uranium. Like a hill, atoms tend to "roll downhill" and release energy, changing their atomic number to do so.*

nuclei, which provide energy for more activation, and keeps continuing. For most elements, this process is not self-sustaining and therefore the reaction is not practically useful. Even for uranium, reaching a self-sustaining fission is very difficult, because the energy, in order to serve as activation for the next series, must be released as neutrons with kinetic energy. If released in other forms, the reaction will stop. This is one of the major obstacles making fission very difficult.

It is also important to emphasize that to use either nuclear fusion or fission as an energy resource, the reaction end-products must be properly disposed of. When uranium fissions, the smaller fragments are often radioactive. These reaction byproducts can

PHYSICS IN THE WORLD: ITER

The international ITER project is a research reactor designed to produce electrical power from nuclear fusion in a safe way to meet the world's growing energy needs (Figure 7.4). The reactor operates at more than 100 million degrees Celsius, which provides the activation energy needed for hydrogen atoms to collide together and fuse into helium atoms, releasing energy. When ITER operates at its full capacity, it is expected to produce more than 500 megawatts of energy. Nuclear fusion produces heat, so this heat energy is turned into electrical energy with less than 100% efficiency due to the Carnot limit.

Figure 7.4 *This research reactor, called the JET (for Joint European Torus) is being used to prepare for building ITER, a joint international research and development project between the United States, the European Union (EU), Russia, Japan, China, India, and South Korea that seeks to demonstrate the scientific and technical feasibility of fusion power.*

What is particularly interesting is that the reaction that powers ITER is very similar to the reaction that creates sunlight inside the Sun. Some of the initial processes that happen inside the Sun are created by "shortcuts" in ITER—for instance, by using water as an input—but the final step that releases energy is the same inside both ITER and the Sun.

Most fusion devices built to date have been very powerful, but due to their short running time, not very energetic. ITER will be built in southern France at an anticipated cost of $12.1 billion. When ITER finally turns on, in about 2015, it will run continuously, making it both powerful and energetic.

form a long-term hazard. When hydrogen fuses, there are also some radioactive byproducts, but they are much less dangerous and much shorter-lived than those of fission.

ENERGY OF FUSION

Helium has a uniquely low potential energy compared to elements nearby. This means that we can get a lot of potential energy just from transforming hydrogen to helium. One kilogram of hydrogen fused to make helium will release an energy of 270 trillion joules. Just how much energy is this?

- It is enough energy to provide a city of 200,000 people with electrical energy for a year.
- It is the energy to launch 22 Statues of Liberty to escape velocity.
- It is the chemical energy in 2 million gallons of gasoline.
- It is the chemical energy in 30 million meals.

CHAPTER 8

Household Energy Use:
43 Kilowatt-Hours

NOW THAT WE HAVE SEEN THE ORIGINS AND APPLICATIONS of energy in the context of physics, we should bring this understanding into the everyday world. Where does our energy come from and where does it go? How much do we use?

Let us start by thinking about the most obvious energy uses in daily life. The two most apparent energy sources are electrical energy in the home and gasoline power in a car. In Table 8.1, we show how much energy of each type the average American consumes.

You may notice that most of your energy consumption is not consumed directly by you. Instead, it comes from all the other activities in the United States—manufacturing, plane flights, and so on. These are, of course, eventually all consumed by people. So, they should really be counted as part of the average energy consumption by American citizens, even if they are not used directly by people.

In fact, this should make us consider where, exactly, the electrical energy comes from in the first place. In the United States,

TABLE 8.1 U.S. Energy Consumption per Capita

TYPE OF ENERGY	KILOWATT-HOURS/DAY
Residential electrical	11.5
Gasoline	28.5
Food	2.3
All other electrical	23.2
All other oil	42.8
Total	108.3

most electrical energy comes from burning coal. Coal burning is not perfectly efficient; in order to generate 1 J of electrical energy, you must transfer 3 J of heat energy out of the coal. This inefficiency is due to the Carnot limit. So, again, though this coal is not directly used by you at home, in order to get the electricity, this much energy had to be used up.

This allows us to calculate how much energy is used in total throughout the power generation chain per person in the United States. This is shown in Table 8.2. The energy amounts are larger now because they account for the heat energy that was wasted while making electricity.

We should also consider, that most of this energy cannot be used for work, due to the Carnot limit. For instance, gasoline is only about 30% efficient in producing work from the heat energy stored in it. Electricity is nearly 100% efficient, at least in principle. Food leads to only about 3% efficiency in conversion of heat energy to work. All the other energy in the entire chain of energy production is lost as heat. The actual mechanical work (kinetic plus potential energy) done, per person per day in the

TABLE 8.2 U.S. Energy Consumption per Capita, Including Energy Sources to Create Electricity	
RAW MATERIALS	**KILOWATT-HOURS/DAY**
Gas	28.5
Coal/Petroleum	74.7
Nuclear	23.1
Hydroelectric	2.4
Food	2.3
Total	131.1

U.S., is about 21 kilowatt-hours (kWh). The remaining 110 kWh of energy that you "consume" actually is lost as heat, unused for any purpose.

Finally, Table 8.3 shows all of these values tabulated for the average human inhabitant on Earth, rather than per American citizen, and then shows the total for the entire United States and the entire world.

There are many interesting conclusions to be drawn by comparing the various numbers in these tables. While you are thinking about them, it may be useful to remember that the United States has about 300 million people and that the population of the entire world is about 6 billion.

There is another important source of energy that you use every day—the food you eat. Food, compared to the other energy uses above, does not directly contribute such a large amount. The food you eat, however, had to be produced using the energy of photosynthesis. In one day, you consume about 2.3 kWh of food energy. In order to produce that energy through photosynthesis and the food chain, more than 17,000 kWh of the Sun's energy is used to produce your food per day.

TABLE 8.3	Energy, Work, and Heat for U.S. and World per Capita and Total	
	AVERAGE INDIVIDUAL (kWh)	**TOTAL (GWh)***
U.S. Consumption/Day	131	39,300
U.S. Heat Loss/Day	110	33,000
U.S. Work/Day	21	6,300
World Consumption/Day	26	157,200
World Heat Loss/Day	22	132,000
World Work/Day	4	25,200
*GWh = Gigawatt-hours (million kilowatt-hours)		

You may be wondering, where does all this energy go that I use every day? The sidebar "Physics and People: Energy Use in the Home," shows the energy consumption of electrical appliances for a typical household of four. You can check the appliances in your home (there is usually a silvery label on appliances giving the information) to see if your family's power consumption is similar.

Do you think you use more or less than this in your household? Are you surprised by the largest electrical users in the home? If you are trying to save energy, which of your appliances are using the most energy and therefore you want to be the most efficient?

SOLAR ENERGY

The ultimate source of most of our energy is, of course, the Sun. It is worth stopping here to clear up a misconception. As the Sun shines on the Earth, the Earth does not get hotter and hotter

PHYSICS AND PEOPLE: Energy Use in the Home

*E*ach appliance in your home lists power consumption in watts. Why not look for yourself at home? It is often on a silver label on the back. The average energy use of each appliance per day is listed in Table 8.4. Of course, appliances like air conditioners are not used every day: Their average use in this table is much lower than the actual average summer use, but higher than the actual average winter use.

Remember, one kilowatt-hour (kWh) is the use of one kilowatt for one hour. This is 1,000 watts × 60 (minutes in an hour) × 60 (seconds in a minute) = 3.6 million joules.

TABLE 8.4   Average Energy Use per Day

APPLIANCE	WATTS	AVG. HOURS/DAY	kWh/DAY
Refrigerator	500	24	12
Water Heater	3,800	3	11.4
Range	12,500	0.5	6.25
Air Conditioning	3,500	1	3.5
Clothes Dryer	5,000	0.5	2.5
Furnace	350	6	2.1

every day. The Earth basically stays the same temperature, with some small variations. This indicates that energy is not building up on Earth. Since the Earth is not cooling down, energy is not leaving the planet either. The energy that leaves the Earth is

APPLIANCE	WATTS	AVG. HOURS/DAY	kWh/DAY
Television	180	6	1.08
Computer (with monitor)	200	5	1
Room Light (3 bulbs)	180	4	0.72
Dishwasher	1,300	0.5	0.65
Chandelier	300	2	0.6
Table Lamp	100	4	0.4
Washing Machine	500	0.5	0.25
Single Bulb	60	4	0.24
Microwave Oven	1,300	0.1	0.13
Ceiling Fan	60	2	0.12
Stereo	30	3	0.09
Coffee Maker	900	0.1	0.09
Vacuum	800	0.1	0.08
Total			43.2

almost exactly equal to the energy that enters it from the Sun (Figure 8.1).

We can see sunlight streaming down from the sky during the day, but it is probably not at all apparent to you how this energy

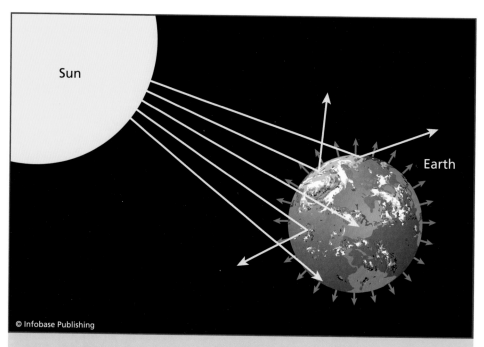

Figure 8.1 *Sunlight carries energy from the Sun to the Earth. Much of the sunlight is simply reflected off of clouds or the planet surface. Most of the rest warms the Earth, which then "glows" with infrared radiation. An exceedingly tiny portion of the Sun's energy is used for photosynthesis, and an even smaller amount is ultimately used for work.*

leaves the Earth. The light from the Sun is in the visible part of the spectrum, a mix of all colors from red to blue that looks white. There are three major ways that energy leaves the Earth. The first is that it never gets here—that is, much of the Sun's light is reflected off the clouds and atmosphere instead of coming to the ground. The second is that it reflects off of icecaps or the ocean after reaching the ground. This is why the Earth, from far away in space, looks like a "pale blue dot" from reflected light. Finally, light that reaches the ground heats up the ground, and the ground emits radiation, glowing with light. An object with a temperature like the Earth (around 250 K), however, glows largely not orange or yellow or blue but instead with infrared light. This is one of the major energy losses of the Earth, and since humans cannot see infrared light, the energy seems to escape invisibly.

There are also a couple of additional minor ways that the Sun's energy is disposed of. A very tiny portion of the Sun's light (less than 1/10,000th) is used in photosynthesis to store potential energy in sugars. This tiny portion is mostly eventually released as heat (which emits more infrared radiation into space), though some of it is used to do work. In the end, all the energy from the Sun (except for the exceedingly minute quantity—less than one-millionth—used to do work) is re-radiated back into space, but in a different form. That is, it is mostly infrared light instead of mostly visible light.

Just how much energy is coming from the Sun? As we discussed earlier, the light power from the Sun is about 1.5 kW through every square meter of area, just at the top of the atmosphere. But only about a third of this light power reaches the ground. So if you set your teacher's desk (with an area of about 2 m^2) outside, at most about 1,000 watts of light energy would be hitting it. Some of that energy would be absorbed by the desktop, and some would be reflected elsewhere.

How much power is incident on the whole Earth? About 2×10^{15} kWh per day. This is approximately 6,600 times larger than the total energy consumption over the entire world. This is very exciting, but is there enough solar power to go around? First of all, the very best devices in the world have only 10% efficiency to convert solar power. This hardly seems problematic—there's still 660 times the needed power.

We can calculate how much area would be needed to supply the world's power consumption, with a 10% efficient device that is in sunlight an average of 12 hours per 24 hour day. It turns out that to fulfill our needs, the entire state of California would have to be covered with solar cell devices. Furthermore, every single year, due to world energy consumption growth, an additional area the size of the entire state of Connecticut would have to be covered with solar devices.

OTHER SOURCES OF ENERGY

The major contributors to our total energy use are oil, coal, and nuclear power, in that order; they account for 57%, 22%, and 20%, respectively, of energy consumption in the United States. Are these related to our major energy source, the Sun?

Coal and oil are known as "fossil fuels" because they come ultimately from living things of the distant past. As fossilized plants and animals became subject to intense pressures far underground, their body elements transformed into oil or coal. Of course, where did these plants and animals get their energy? The plants got it from photosynthesizing the light of the Sun, and the animals got it from eating the plants. Thus, these fuels are really stored solar energy.

The fossil fuels we use today consist of energy from our Sun, created slowly over hundreds of millions of years underground, and then stored as potential chemical energy for hundreds of millions of years more. It is likely that humans will use up this entire store of fossil fuels in less than 1,000 years.

Is nuclear power from the Sun? Not at all. The two kinds of nuclear power—fission and fusion—come from different sources. Energy from nuclear fission is potential energy that was stored in uranium nuclei during their creation. When and where were uranium nuclei created? They were created billions of years ago during explosions of stars known as supernovae. When these supernovae burst, uranium atoms spewed across the galaxy. Some of them eventually came to rest in the disk of dust around the Sun that, billions of years ago, turned into the Earth and other planets. When we generate energy from nuclear fission, we are using energy created in star explosions and stored for billions of years.

Nuclear fusion is precisely the process by which energy is created in the Sun. If and when nuclear fusion power plants function on Earth, they will be like a miniature source of solar power. So, where does the energy in nuclear fusion (and therefore, solar power) come from?

Fusion of hydrogen nuclei is not spontaneous because it requires a very high activation energy. Stars are places where the

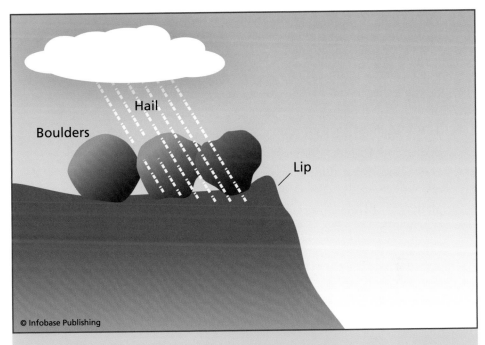

Figure 8.2 *Boulders at the top of a cliff with a lip. If hail from a sudden storm were to provide one of the rocks with enough energy to bounce over the lip, tremendous energy could be released.*

initial activation energy is provided by gravitational attraction; the first few fusions then provide enough energy for additional fusion and the reaction becomes self-sustaining. Luckily, because it is not spontaneous, there are still many hydrogen and helium nuclei left "unburned" in the universe. Eventually, all the nuclei in the universe will be nickel-59, but we are not there yet. There is plenty of fuel yet.

And why should hydrogen, when burned through fusion, create energy? Is this a storage of energy from long ago? No, hydrogen atoms are like balls poised on a cliff, ready to fall, but not yet fallen (Figure 8.2).

They require an activation energy to get rolling downhill; they are near the edge of a cliff, but the cliff has a lip. And so far, the lip has prevented most of the hydrogen in the universe from fusing into helium, or from there yet higher into other elements.

The energy released when hydrogen nuclei fuse together is due to the delicate balance of the strong nuclear force and quantum mechanics. Why the strong force is the way it is, and why quantum mechanics is the way it is, these are simply mysteries. The shining of the Sun, however, shows how fortune has smiled upon us, in so delicate an arrangement.

CHAPTER 9

Conclusion

WE HAVE COME A LONG WAY IN OUR UNDERSTANDING OF energy. We have seen how by considering force acting over a distance, we can do work and enhance the potential or kinetic energy of an object. We put this together with an understanding of heat. These basics, in turn, allowed us to carefully inquire about electrical energy, chemical energy, and nuclear energy. We can now understand the relations of these types of energies to one another, and understand the role of energy transfer, storage, and heat transfer efficiency. These are all crucial to understanding the role of energy in everyday life.

We have also seen, in each chapter, examples of typical energy quantities. These may often guide you in cases where you might find yourself wondering or guessing how much energy something has. For instance, kinetic energies of everyday objects are often thousands or occasionally millions of joules; gravitational potential energy of large buildings is often megajoules; and similarly for chemical binding energies in materials or electrical energy in battery storage. Now, you can find ways to apply what you've learned and read to your everyday life.

The management of the Earth's energy resources is likely to be one of the most important world issues over your lifetime. You are going to be responsible for your own energy use, and for participating constructively in discussions of how to save energy. Nature has put very strict rules on our use of energy—it is not free, and it can't be created. Within these physical constraints, you should think seriously about what you can do.

GLOSSARY

ACTIVATION ENERGY A small amount of energy required to start a reaction that would not have been spontaneous.

ATOMIC NUMBER The number of protons in an atom.

BALLISTICS The study of the path of projectiles after they have been released.

BINDING ENERGY The energy required to break something apart into its constituents. Binding energy is a signal of negative potential energy with respect to the separated configuration.

BOLTZMANN'S CONSTANT A number with the value 1.4×10^{-23} J/K, which is used to determine the relation between temperature and the energy of a single molecule.

BTU (BRITISH THERMAL UNIT) A unit of energy equal to 1,055 joules.

CALORIE A unit of energy equal to 4,168 joules. When written uncapitalized as calorie, it is equal to 4.168 joules.

CARNOT LIMIT The maximum possible efficiency with which heat energy may be transformed into work. The value depends on the surrounding temperatures during the conversion.

CHARGE The measure of how a particle participates in electrical interactions. If the charge is neutral (zero), then it does not participate in electrical interactions. If it is positive, it attracts negative charges and repels positive charges. If it is negative, it attracts positive and repels negative charges. The magnitude of the charge tells how strong the attraction or repulsion will be. The smallest amount of charge possible is the charge on a proton or electron. The SI unit for charge is the coulomb (C). The charge of one electron is 1.6×10^{-19} coulomb.

CHEMICAL ENERGY The potential energy that can be released by allowing chemical constituents to bond. The energy is released primarily as heat.

CONDUCTION The transfer of heat by objects in direct contact, due to the collision of their molecules.

CONSERVATION In physics, when the total of some quantity must always remain the same, there is a law of "conservation." For instance, because energy cannot be created or destroyed, the total amount of it must always be the same; therefore, we call it "conservation of energy."

CONVECTION The transfer of heat by moving hot or cold objects, usually liquids (like water) or gases (like air.)

COULOMB (C) A unit of electrical charge. One coulomb is equal to the charge of 6.2×10^{18} protons.

DELTA (Δ) The Greek letter "d," this sign often stands for "difference." So, for instance, if *h2* is the height of the roof of a house and *h1* is the height of the doorstep, the difference in height is signified with $\Delta h = h2 - h1$.

DISPLACEMENT Refers to the distance and direction an object has moved in going from one spot to another.

ELECTRICAL POTENTIAL The potential energy per coulomb in a particular electrical configuration. To find the potential energy, multiply the electrical potential by the number of coulombs of charge.

ELECTRICITY The interaction of particles with electric charge.

ELECTRON The lightest elementary particle, which resides in atomic orbitals outside the nucleus. The electron has a negative electric charge, which is why it is attracted to the positively charged protons in the nucleus. The electron is much lighter than protons or neutrons.

ELECTRON VOLT (eV) The energy obtained by one electron moving through an electrical potential difference of one volt. Since 1 volt is 1 joule/coulomb, and one electron is 1.6×10^{-19} C, 1 eV is 1.6×10^{-19} J. This unit of energy is very convenient in particle physics or chemistry, when single electrons at a time are being considered.

ENDOTHERMIC A chemical reaction that must absorb energy, usually from its surroundings, in order to take place. Endothermic reactions usually absorb heat.

ENERGY A quantity that must always have the same total, never altered or destroyed. It can be manifested as motion, potential, electrical or chemical potential, or heat.

ESCAPE VELOCITY Velocity sufficient to escape the gravitational field of Earth without any further need for propulsion.

EXOTHERMIC   A chemical reaction that produces net energy when it takes place.

FISSION   The process of splitting a nucleus into smaller nuclei. This can release potential energy if the original nucleus is large enough.

FORCE   Mass times acceleration. Force is a vector quantity.

FUSION   The process of combining small nuclei into bigger ones. This can release potential energy if the original nuclei are small enough.

g   The standard symbol for the acceleration of gravity at the Earth's surface: 9.8 m/s^2.

GAMMA RAY   A form of very high-energy (short-wavelength) light. It usually comes from nuclear decays or interactions.

GRAVITATIONAL POTENTIAL ENERGY   Potential energy that is due to the position of an object in a gravitational field.

GROUND STATE   In chemistry or nuclear physics, when several particles or nuclei come together, the distance and configuration they can come together into that has the lowest possible potential energy.

HEAT   Transfer of energy that is due to a difference of temperature, from hot to cold.

INELASTIC COLLISION   The kind of collision in which the total kinetic energy afterwards is less than the kinetic energy before.

INFRARED (IR)   A form of light not visible to the human eye, with wavelengths longer than visible light. Many objects give off much infrared light due to thermal radiation, and human skin perceives infrared light as heat.

JOULE (J)   The basic unit of energy; 1 joule is $1 \text{ kg m}^2/\text{s}^2$, or 1 newton-meter.

KELVIN   A unit of measuring degrees of temperature. One kelvin is the same size as one degree Celsius, but $0°$ Celsius equals 273.15 kelvins.

KINETIC ENERGY   Energy that an object has due solely to its state of motion.

LIGHT   A general term covering many different kinds of electromagnetic waves. The wavelength of the waves determines the color or kind of light. Visible light has wavelengths from 450 nm (violet) to 800 nm (red). Other kinds of light at longer wavelengths are infrared, radio, and microwave; at shorter wavelengths are ultraviolet, X-ray, and gamma rays.

MICROWAVE   A form of light with wavelengths longer than about 1 cm.

NEUTRON   An electrically neutral particle, nearly equal in mass to the proton, which is also found in the nucleus with protons.

NEWTON   The unit of force. One newton is equal to a mass of 1 kg accelerated at 1 m/s^2.

NUCLEUS   The central core of an atom, containing electrically neutral neutrons and electrically positive protons. The positive charge of the protons holds the electrons in their orbitals.

PERIOD OF TIME   For a rotating object, the amount of time it takes for one complete revolution.

POTENTIAL ENERGY   Energy that comes about because a particular configuration has been achieved, either by doing work or by reducing kinetic energy.

POWER   The rate of transfer of energy from one form or object to another. It is the energy transferred divided by the time the transfer takes. Power is usually measured in watts, or joules per second.

PROTON   A positively charged particle, much more massive than the electron, that is found in the nucleus of an atom.

RADIATION   The emission of energy in the form of waves or particles.

RELATIVITY   Albert Einstein's theory of how objects behave at very high velocities. The most important result is that the mass of an object contributes to its energy, and this energy may be converted to other forms if the mass changes. In relativity, the mass is no longer permanently fixed.

SPECIFIC HEAT CAPACITY   The amount of heat it takes to heat one kilogram of an object by one degree Celsius.

SPEED   The magnitude of velocity. It is the same regardless of direction.

STRONG NUCLEAR FORCE The force that holds protons together inside a nucleus despite their electrical repulsion. It is a different kind of force from electricity or gravity. It also holds neutrons in the nucleus.

TEMPERATURE A measure of the average amount of random kinetic energy each molecule of an object possesses.

THERMAL ENERGY The sum of all the random kinetic energy of all molecules in an object. The amount of thermal energy is related to the temperature.

THERMODYNAMICS The study of processes that involve heat.

ULTRAVIOLET (UV) A form of light not visible to the human eye, with shorter wavelength than visible light.

VELOCITY The vector representing not only the speed of an object but also its direction.

VOLTS The unit of electrical potential. An electrical potential difference of one volt means that as one coulomb of charge is moved, it changes its potential energy by one joule.

WATT A measure of power. One watt is equivalent to one joule per second.

WAVELENGTH The distance between one crest and the next in a wave. Light is a kind of wave, and the wavelength of the light determines its color (if it is visible light) or its kind (if it is not visible light; i.e., ultraviolet, infrared, X-ray, etc.).

WORK The transfer of energy to an object (either potential or kinetic) by imposing a force over a distance.

X-RAY A form of light not visible to the human eye, with very short wavelengths, shorter than ultraviolet but longer than gamma rays.

BIBLIOGRAPHY

Cahn, Robert, and Gerson Goldhaber. *The Experimental Foundations of Particle Physics*. New York: Cambridge University Press, 1989.

Dunlap, Richard. *The Physics of Nuclei and Particles*. Belmont, Calif.: Thomson Brooks/Cole, 2004.

Elert, Glenn. "Chemical Energy." *The Physics Hypertextbook Web site*. http://hypertextbook.com/physics/matter/energy-chemical/.

Faraday, Michael. *The Chemical History of a Candle*. Mineola, N.Y.: Dover Publications, 2003.

Feynman, Richard F. *The Feynman Lectures on Physics, Vol. I*. Redwood City, Calif.: Addison-Wesley/Longman, 1970.

Feynman, Richard F. *QED: The Strange Theory of Light and Matter*. Princeton, N.J.: Princeton University Press, 1988.

Giancoli, Douglas. *Physics*. Upper Saddle River, N.J.: Prentice-Hall, 2004.

Lide, David. CRC *Handbook of Chemistry and Physics*. Boca Raton, Fla.: CRC Press, 2004.

Purcell, Ed. *Electricity and Magnetism*. New York: McGraw-Hill, 1970.

Sherman, Gabriel. "Maximum Velocity." *Popular Science*, February 2005.

FURTHER READING

Adair, Robert. *The Physics of Baseball*. New York: Harper, 2002.

Faraday, Michael. *The Chemical History of a Candle*. Mineola, N.Y.: Dover Publications, 2003.

Feynman, Richard F. *The Feynman Lectures on Physics, Vol. I.* Redwood City, Calif.: Addison-Wesley/Longman, 1970.

Feynman, Richard F. *Six Easy Pieces*. Reading, Mass.: Perseus, 1996.

Freeman, Ian. *Physics Made Simple*. New York: Made Simple Press, 1989.

Giancoli, Douglas. *Physics*. Upper Saddle River, N.J.: Prentice-Hall, 2004.

Hinrichs, Roger, and Merlin Kleinbach. *Energy: Its Use and the Environment*. Fort Worth, Texas: Brooks/Cole, 2001.

Krauss, Lawrence M. *The Physics of Star Trek*. New York: Harper, 1996.

March, Robert. *Physics for Poets*. New York: McGraw-Hill, 1995.

Sherman, Gabriel. "Maximum Velocity." *Popular Science*, February 2005.

Smil, Vaclav. *Energies: An Illustrated Guide to the Biosphere and Civilization*. Cambridge, Mass.: MIT Press, 2000.

Smil, Vaclav. *Energy in World History*. Boulder, Colo.: Westview Press, 1994.

Smith, Crosbie. *The Science of Energy*. Chicago: University of Chicago Press, 1999.

Walker, Jearl. *The Flying Circus of Physics (with Answers)*. New York: Wiley, 1977.

Web Sites

Amusement Park Physics
http://www.learner.org/exhibits/parkphysics/

Ask a Scientist: Physics
http://www.newton.dep.anl.gov/askasci/phys98.htm

Flash Animations for Physics
http://www.upscale.utoronto.ca/GeneralInterest/Harrison/Flash/

History of Physics and Astronomy
http://www.physlink.com/Education/History.cfm

How Things Work: Explaining the Physics of Everyday Life
http://howthingswork.virginia.edu/home.html

Institute of Physics
http://www.iop.org

Live the Physics
http://library.thinkquest.org/13526/index3.htm

Physics Classroom
http://www.physicsclassroom.com

Physics Web
http://physicsweb.org

Physics 2000
http://www.colorado.edu/physics/2000/index.pl

Picture Credits

INDEX

A

Acceleration, 20
    formulas, 26
    of gravity, 36, 40
Activation energy
    release of, 45–49, 95–96,
       107
Antifreeze, 63
Armstrong, Lance, 19
Atomic number, 93

B

Ballistics
    studies of, 37–40
Batteries
    advances in, 74
    energy storage of, 16,
       74–76, 85, 109
    volts and work, 12, 71
Bernoulli, Daniel, 25
Bikes
    and kinetic energy, 19, 24,
       32–34
Binding energy, 95, 97
    and chemical bonds, 80,
       82, 109
    electrical, 73, 93
    gravitational, 45
    total, 94
Boltzmann's constant, 54
British thermal unit. *See* BTU
BTU (British thermal unit),
   11
    measurement of, 12, 15

C

Calorie
    defined, 12
    measurement of chemical
      substances, 13
    measurement of heat, 13
    and temperature, 12

Car engine
    coolant system, 63
    electrical energy, 75–76,
      86,
Carnot limit
    electrical energy, 96, 99
    work energy, 56, 62–63,
      86
Charcoal
    and heat energy, 58, 60
Chemical energy, 8, 97
    bonds, 80–84, 109
    energy levels in, 77–80,
      109
    formulas, 85
    and heat, 13, 61–62
    measurement, 13
    origins of, 61
    reactions, 82–83, 85–86
Coal, 106–108
    energy, 99
Collisions, 8
    inelastic, 31
    and kinetic energy, 27–28,
      30–31
Combustion, 61
Conduction
    and heat transfer, 57–58,
      63
Conservation
    of electrical energy, 67,
      110
    and the exchange theorem,
      9
    of kinetic energy, 27,
      38–39, 91
    laws of, 8, 10–11, 19, 25
    of momentum, 11, 28, 30,
      91
Convection
    and heat transfer, 57–58
Conversions, 14

Coulomb (C)
of charge, 69, 71, 73
Coulomb, Charles de, 69

D
Definition
of energy, 7–10
Delta
changes with, 21
Displacement, 22–23
times a force, 37
Distance
maximum, 40
measurement, 27
vector, 22–23

E
Einstein, Albert, 11
theory of relativity, 87,
89–91
Electricity, 7–8
charges, 65, 68–69, 71, 73,
96, 109
force, 66, 77, 82, 93
household, 15, 52, 85,
97–98, 101–103
measurement, 73, 96
rules of, 78
sources, 99
stored potential,
67–69, 71, 73, 77,
82–84
transformation, 18, 47
use per capita, 100
Electrons
charged energy of, 12,
68–69, 71, 73
configuration changes,
77–81
detached, 65–68
energy levels, 77–78, 80,
82, 84, 93

Electron volt (eV), 85
motion of atoms and
molecules, 12–13, 71
Electrostatic forces, 71
Endothermic reactions, 82
Escape velocity
energy of, 44–45, 51, 76,
85, 97
Exchange theorem, 9–10
Exothermic reactions, 82

F
Feynman, Richard
*QED: The Strange Theory of
Light and Matter,* 10
Fission
nuclear, 106
process of, 93–95, 97
self-sustaining, 95
uranium, 95
Food
chemical energy of, 61,
99–100
Forces, 7
calculation formulas, 24,
26
electrical, 66, 71, 77, 82,
93
direction, 23, 45, 56, 109
gravitational, 21, 36–37,
67–68
measurement, 20–21
strong nuclear, 93, 108
vector, 22
Friction
air resistance, 18, 39–40
brakes, 29
heat, 65
Fusion
devices, 93–96
energy of, 97
helium, 96–97, 107–108

hydrogen, 94, 96–97,
106–108
nuclear, 94, 96, 106

G
Gamma rays, 59
emitted, 9
Gas
chemical energy of, 61, 85,
97–98
thermal energy of, 16,
53–54
Geothermal energy, 52
Glucose
reactions, 84–85
Grand Canyon, 15
Gravitational
attraction, 107
fields, 46, 51
formulas, 46
potential energy, 36–37,
43, 66, 68–69, 109
pull of the sun, 45
Ground state, 78, 80

H
Hammers
and kinetic energy,
33–34
Heat energy, 8, 42
capacity, 62
and chemistry, 61–62
defined, 55–56
and friction, 65
latent, 55
and light, 58–61
measurement, 13, 15
potential, 86
of the sun, 52–64
transfer, 15, 18, 29, 31, 37,
47, 55–58, 61–63, 76,
82–84, 99–100, 109

use per capita, 101
waste, 16
Helium
fusion, 96–97, 107–108
neutrons, 93
Horsepower
consumption, 15
Household energy
electricity, 15, 85, 98,
101–103
per capita, 99
use, 52, 98–108, 64, 76,
98, 101–103
Huxley, Thomas, 17
Hydrogen atoms
and activation energy,
96
energy level, 77–78,
80–82, 93
forms, 94
fusion, 94, 96–97,
106–108

I
Infrared light, 8, 83
and heat energy, 59–61,
105
vision, 61
ITER, 96

J
Joule (J), 35–52
calculation formulas, 14,
24, 26, 33
compound unit, 20
defined, 22
of energy, 69, 71, 73, 75,
97, 99, 102, 109
and mechanical energy, 13,
16, 29–30
official energy unit, 11–13,
15, 20

K

Kelvin scale, 54, 56, 62
Kinetic energy
    calculation formulas,
        18–21, 25–28, 31–33,
        35, 39
    and collisions, 27–28,
        30–31
    conservation of, 27
    measurement of, 26–28,
        31–33, 35, 39, 46,
        52–55, 87, 89
    of a roller coaster, 29
    of rotation, 31–32
    and skaters, bikes and
        hammers, 33–34
    studies of, 37–40
    transformation, 15, 18, 29,
        35–37, 39, 46, 55–57,
        84, 89, 93–94, 99,
        109
    and work, 23–26, 42–44,
        67
    zero, 29, 35

L

Lifting
    and work, 42–44
Light
    absorption, 61, 64, 84
    and color, 59–60
    energy, 8, 16, 94, 105
    forms of, 59, 83
    and heat, 58
    infrared, 8, 59, 60–61, 83,
        105
    reflection, 84
    solar, 62, 64, 84,
        104–105
    speed of, 46–47
    ultraviolet, 59–60, 83
    waves, 58–60

Light bulbs
    brightness, 15
    energy use, 15, 52
    incandescent, 58

M

Mass
    affects on, 94
    lost, 94
    measurement in kilograms,
        19, 26–28, 31–32,
        35–36, 62, 69, 74
    propel, 92
Measurement
    of collisions, 27–28
    of direction of motion,
        22–23
    of energy, 8, 10–13
    of force formulas,
        22–24
    of joule formulas, 14
    of kinetic energy, 18–21,
        26–27, 87
    of kinetic energy formulas,
        19–20, 25–28, 31–33,
        35, 39, 46, 53–54
    and lifting, 42
    of maximum height, 46
    of potential energy
        formulas, 46, 49, 66,
        71, 73, 75, 78
    of power, 15–16
    of projectiles, 40
    of relativity, formulas, 87,
        89–91, 94
    of thermal energy, 54, 56
    units, 11–16, 19–20, 75
    of velocity, 19, 26–28, 31,
        39, 47, 92
    of voltage differences, 71,
        73
    of watt formulas, 14, 75

of work, 21, 24, 36, 43,
 73, 75
Mechanical energy, 8, 12
 measurement, 13, 42–43
 and work, 56, 86
Microwaves, 59, 83
Motion
 direction, 22
 energy of, 33

N

Neutrons
 and helium, 93
 of hydrogen, 94
Newton
 compound unit, 20, 22
Newton, Isaac, 25, 37
Noether, Emmy
 and energy conservation,
 10–11
Noether's theorem, 11
Nuclear energy, 8
 energy, 106–108
 fission, 106
 force, 108
 fusion, 94, 96, 106
Nuclear physics, 77
Nuclear power plants, 94

O

Oil, 8
 household use, 52, 106
 reserves, 16

P

Pauli, Wolfgang
 exchange theorem, 9–10
Photosynthesis, 100
Physicist
 problems, 21, 25
 theories, 9–12, 37
 thinking about energy,
 16–17

Potential energy, 8
 chemical, 83–84
 defined, 35–36, 68
 difference, 40, 42, 49,
 66–67, 69, 71, 73, 75
 electrical, 37, 67–69, 71,
 77, 82–83
 gravitational, 36, 45, 69,
 109
 measurement of, 40, 42,
 46, 66, 69, 75, 78
 of a roller coaster, 29
 stored, 68, 84
 studies of, 37–40
 transformation, 15, 18, 29,
 39, 46–47, 55–56, 93,
 97, 99, 109
 and work, 36–37, 42–45,
 66–67, 74–75
 zero-point of, 29, 40, 42,
 48, 68, 78, 80
Power
 defined, 15
 and energy changing form,
 15
 measurement of, 15–16
Protons
 charged, 65–66, 68–69,
 71, 73
 energy levels, 77–82, 93
 of hydrogen, 94

Q

QED: The Strange Theory of
 Light and Matter (Feynman),
 10
Quantum mechanics, 78,
 108

R

Radiation, 8
 byproducts, 97
 decay of elements, 9